History of the Mission House of the Protestant Episcopal Church in the United States

Samuel Durborow

Nabu Public Domain Reprints:

You are holding a reproduction of an original work published before 1923 that is in the public domain in the United States of America, and possibly other countries. You may freely copy and distribute this work as no entity (individual or corporate) has a copyright on the body of the work. This book may contain prior copyright references, and library stamps (as most of these works were scanned from library copies). These have been scanned and retained as part of the historical artifact.

This book may have occasional imperfections such as missing or blurred pages, poor pictures, errant marks, etc. that were either part of the original artifact, or were introduced by the scanning process. We believe this work is culturally important, and despite the imperfections, have elected to bring it back into print as part of our continuing commitment to the preservation of printed works worldwide. We appreciate your understanding of the imperfections in the preservation process, and hope you enjoy this valuable book.

P. E. Foreign Mission House, West Philadelphia, Pa.

HISTORY

OF THE

MISSION HOUSE

OF THE

PROTESTANT EPISCOPAL CHURCH, IN THE UNITED STATES.

PRINTED WITH THE APPROVAL OF THE BOARD OF MANAGERS.

MISSION HOUSE LOCATED IN W. PHILADELPHIA,
No. 3518 Lancaster Avenue.

TREASURER,
CHARLES B. DURBOROW, Esq.
No. 234 Market Street, Philadelphia.

PHILADELPHIA:
A. C. BRYSON & CO., PRINTERS, 607 CHESTNUT STREET.
1869.

Educ 6181.16.50

1871, April 25.
Gift of
Rev. William Stevens Perry,
of Geneva, N.Y.
(H.U. 1854.)

HISTORY OF THE MISSION HOUSE

OF THE

Protestant Episcopal Church.

UNTIL a comparatively recent period the supply of Missionaries for the Foreign field, was drawn from students educated at the Theological Seminaries in the course of studies designed to prepare them for parochial ministrations; or from the ranks of the clergy already in Holy Orders, who had not, at the time of their ordination, entertained the idea of preaching the gospel to the heathen in foreign lands. Within a few years, however, the inadequacy of the supply, and the unfitness of some who were willing to serve, has aroused the friends of foreign missions to the urgent necessity of taking proper steps to increase the number of foreign missionaries; and to give them, beforehand, that special training which would fit them to labor successfully in their respective fields.

Two plans were suggested: one, the foundation at each Divinity School, of a Professorship of Missionary Training; the other, the establishment of a special institution, to give the requisite education and training to the young men in whose hearts God's Holy Spirit might implant a desire to go abroad, and preach the Gospel of His Blessed Son to the benighted and perishing heathen.

On this latter plan this institution was organized. It recognizes as a fundamental basis, the idea that men designed to engage in a *special Missionary work* like that of the foreign field,—*require special training.*

Although such an institution, before this organization was completed, was wholly unknown in the United States, the abundant success which had attended similar institutions in Europe, made it evident that it was by far the most feasible plan. The Missionary College at Basle, Switzerland, founded about fifty years since, is engaged in educating men to be foreign Missionaries. It has trained and sent out upwards of four hundred messengers of the Good Tidings, who, in various zones and climates of the globe, and in connection with various Protestant Missionary organizations, have labored most zealously and successfully. In England, the Church Missionary College, at Islington; St. Augustine's Missionary College, Canterbury; and St. Aidan's College, Birkenhead; are devoted specially to the education of young men, to be properly prepared and qualified Missionaries in foreign countries. Though none of them are yet old institutions, their success has been most encouraging, and the Church Missionary College alone, has furnished some three hundred clergy for the foreign field.

On the other part, the college of the "*Congregatio de Propaganda Fide,*" instituted in Rome, in 1622, has been devoted to the special work of educating men to spread Romanism among the heathen.

These were some of the facts and considerations

which led to the establishment of the institution, known successively by the titles of the "EPISCOPAL MISSIONARY TRAINING SCHOOL," the "GAMBIER MISSION HOUSE," and the "MISSION HOUSE OF THE PROTESTANT EPISCOPAL CHURCH," in the United States. We proceed in the following pages, to give a connected and somewhat detailed account of the history of this Missionary establishment of the Church, drawn from the minutes, and from various other sources.

ORIGIN OF THE MISSION HOUSE.

1863.

The first movement towards the organization was made by the REV. J. G. AUER,* one of the Missionaries of the Protestant Episcopal Church, in Liberia; but at this date absent on leave in the United States. Both his own education at Basle, and his experience as Missionary in Africa, made him feel very much the want of a special Missionary school in the United States, and soon after his return from Africa he began to prepare the minds of churchmen to feel with him. The very first step taken by him to call *public attention* to the subject, was the delivery of a course of Special Missionary Lectures, in the lecture-room of the Church

---

* NOTE.—The Rev. J. G. AUER was educated at the Basle Missionary College, and afterwards engaged in the Basle Mission on the Gold Coast. He became a candidate for Holy Orders in the Protestant Episcopal Church, and in February, 1862, he was ordained by Bishop PAYNE, and appointed to Bohlen Station, Liberia.

He is a gentleman of much practical experience, filled with burning zeal in the cause of Missions, and is one of our most diligent and successful Foreign Missionaries.

of the Epiphany, Philadelphia, in behalf of such a school, on November 2d, 3d, 4th and 5th, 1863.

Bishop POTTER, Bishop STEVENS, and other eminent clergy, and laymen, advocated the plan warmly. A contribution of about $100 was made in the Church of the Epiphany, and $20 by Emmanuel Church, Kensington, Philadelphia. Mr. AUER, as Agent of the Foreign Committee of the Board of Missions, had to travel through the Western Dioceses. At Gambier he also emptied his heart concerning a Mission House, first to Bishop BEDELL, and afterwards to the clergy at Gambier. Bishop McILVAINE, then in the east, hailed the enterprise with joy, and gave the full weight of his influence to bring it to life. A little before this, Bishop PAYNE in Africa, to whom the plan had been communicated, expressed his sympathy with the movement.

Even then it was asked whether the institution should be located at Gambier, or Philadelphia. The Gambier friends had the advantages of concentration and easy organization; while the clergy of Philadelphia were less easily brought together, and at the time, had their hands full with the newly-established Divinity School, Episcopal Hospital, Christian Commission, &c. Thus Gambier acquired the honor of being the *Cradle of the Mission House.*

In November, 1863, Mr. AUER, addressed a letter to Bishop BEDELL, suggesting the advantage and practicability of establishing a Mission House in the United States, from which we quote the following portions:

"A Seminary for Training Foreign Missionaries in this country, did not meet the approbation of the Foreign Committee in New York. They think it would be impossible to establish one regarding both means and men. I, of course, cannot go on in speaking on the subject and interesting the church at large; but as long as we have so great need of *more laborers*, and as it is very unlikely that we shall get a sufficient number of efficient Missionaries from our Theological Seminaries, I cannot but pray the Lord of the Harvest to open new channels for procuring laborers; and I shall, in private circles, speak of this matter until I am forbidden to do so. I hope that if our treasury is in a better state when the Five Cent collection begins to bear fruit,—and it is beginning to do so,—the committee will be less afraid to enter into the plan.

"One thing is clear,—we have not sufficient Missionaries.* What are two men from this increasing Episcopal Church, for Africa? Our students will not go * * * * * *. Other countries and Missionary Societies *have* sufficient laborers, and they have men who do not run away again, as a number of ours did in China and Africa. But they do *not* get them from universities and ministers; at least, if they get *them*, it is an exception, not the rule. The Church Missionary Society in England used to be obliged to get two or more

---

* NOTE.—From 1859 to 1867 only two Theological Students from Church Educational Institutions, went out as Foreign Missionaries, and the increasing scarcity of candidates for this department of the Church's work, has almost stripped the various stations bare of Missionaries from this country.

Missionaries from Basle every year; but since 1858 they have been able to do without that supply, as they have about fifty students from Great Britain in the Missionary College at Islington. There are strong young men in *this* country, with a warm heart for missions, who have not sufficient education, no means, no friends, to enter a college or seminary; they cannot so much as think of studying for the Missionary work. Let us have a seminary where they will be admitted just as they are, and educated without any expense on their part, and it will be a powerful call to many. Then we shall train them in a Missionary spirit, they will not change their minds when tempting positions offer; they will go,—go for life, and will rather die on the field if they cannot live.

"Our Protestant Episcopal Church has as much life as any, or more. Why then have we no more Missionaries? If we cannot fill our dark places in Africa with at least two Missionaries each, it is killing those few that labor there; and still the heathen cry in vain, *'give us more teachers!'* Should not all this open our eyes, that we have not yet hit upon the right way of procuring Missionaries and of carrying on the work? Monthly Concerts or Missionary Prayer Meetings ought to be held for diffusing more Missionary spirit, which is the Spirit of Jesus, from Whom the seven spirits go out into all lands; and we ought to have a Missionary Seminary at home. The brethren in Philadelphia are in favor of this; Bishop POTTER recommended it after one of my lectures. If only somebody would take the matter in hand, it would prosper. Without Jesus we can do nothing. He must put it into the hearts of ministers and people to work and to pray. Oh! that the church would pray more that Missionary-prayer to the Lord of the Harvest for more laborers."

This letter, and the continued earnest agitation of the subject by Mr. AUER, awakened an interest in this matter in various quarters. The subject was so novel that some were doubtful, and, as is likely to be the case in regard to any new enterprise, many were indifferent. It was proposed to attempt the establishment of a Missionary Training School, at Gambier, Knox County, Ohio, in the vicinity of the Theological institutions of that Diocese, which are located there. The Rev. Mr. AUER, addressed a second letter to Bishop BEDELL on the subject as follows:—

1864.

PHILADELPHIA, May 2, 1864.

DEAR BISHOP:—

* * * * * * If we have not a very particular and specific Missionary School, we shall not be able to carry on the work already began, as it ought to be, if we want to prosper. This afternoon I happily met Bishop MCILVAINE, and told him of the brethen's proceedings at Gambier, and your opinion about it. He at once entered into our plans for Gambier, with great joy. He has no doubt that sufficient land will be granted at Gambier, and that the Western spirit will be rather more favorable for the school then the East. I was surprised to hear him wish that the Mission School might be entirely independent of any other school or seminary,—only that would be too expensive to obtain and to maintain. My whole impression is now, that all these are plain indications that we ought to choose Gambier; for it would take long and much to get as many influential brethren *here*, to do what at Gambier and for that place is already done. Willing hearts are God's gifts, and we must use them in time. We need such a Mission School:—

I. To get a ready supply of Missionaries.

II. To get men educated in that one direction and spirit.

III. To get men proved and approved as suited for the work. So often young men begin to study somewhere with the desire to go to the heathen, and by and by they are drawn aside from that purpose and desire. Such cases I have met with in New York, and all other places. And so often young men go out, and get tired of the work, or are not suited. The Foreign Committee has no opportunity to test them before they are sent.

IV. We need a home for Missionaries. I have met cases where Missionaries, (returned on leave from their stations,) have been homeless, and did not know where to go.

V. We need a central fire-place for cultivating, concentrating and diffusing warm Missionary-life; something concrete, that plainly tells the Church what we are about.

Such a Missionary School, wherever it be, will get such a central influence through its teachers and students, correspondence, visits, excursions, perhaps a good Missionary paper, kept and made fresh by correspondence with Foreign Missionaries in all lands. It certainly will draw forth the attention and sympathy of the Church, and even people outside the Church,—at least such is the case with every one in Europe,—and, being established in the very particular sense of the command "go ye into all the world," it will have the sympathy and guidance and protection and blessing of our risen Saviour. I feel—before the Lord—assured that we are now on the right path, and that you, with the brethren at Gambier, with the council and help of Bishop McIlvaine, and any other parties you may desire to help, can do nothing better than go forward in God's name. Let us, however, have no mere formal organization in order to get influence and money: no committee of absent members, no life-members on account of a certain sum of money. There must be order, but the Bishop and Assistant Bishop of the Diocese in which the Mission School shall be located, and a few men of spirit on the spot, can easily arrange the plan of education, and watch over the progress of the Institution. I think the principal cause of success at Basle and Islington, (London,) is, that these schools are chiefly private undertakings of a few. The work of Harms at Hermannsburg, Wichern at Hamburg, Fliedner at Kaiserswerth, and Spittler at Basle proves it emphatically, that God's Spirit works best and most remarkably where the machinery is simple, and the aim decided. (Compare David's sling and Saul's armor.)

This, however, will not, and cannot, prevent the Institution from being an institution of the whole Protestant Episcopal Church, Low and High, East and West, North and South. The above-named undertakings prove this * * * *. I have a special gift to do pioneer-work, but scarcely more; the managers must not forget it, and therefore in good time secure my return to Africa, where such work is still plentiful.

With respectful love, yours humbly,

J. G. AUER.

To Rt. Rev. G. T. BEDELL, D. D.
   Through Rev. A. M. MORRISON.

ORGANIZATION OF THE EPISCOPAL MISSIONARY TRAINING SCHOOL, AT GAMBIER, OHIO.

1864.—May.

Gambier was finally selected as the place where the experiment of establishing a Mission House should be attempted. After a long discussion at a meeting of the Foreign Committee held in New York, in June, the committee gave consent to Rev. Mr. AUER, to prolong his stay in the United States for two years, for the purpose of assisting in the inauguration of the enterprise. The actual progress of the movement can best be seen by the following extracts from the minutes of the proceedings at Gambier:

GAMBIER, OHIO, May 12th, 1864.

"Bishop BEDELL, having desired a meeting of gentlemen to consider a letter from Rev. J. G. AUER, relating to the establishment, at Gambier, Ohio, of a Missionary Training School, such a meeting was held to-day at the residence of the Rev. WM. NEWTON. The following gentlemen were present:—Bishop BEDELL, Rev. Messrs. NEWTON, BLAKE, BANCROFT, McELHINNEY, TULLIDGE, NEFF, MORRISON, and President SHORT, of Kenyon College. After reading Mr. AUER's letter, Bishop BEDELL, appointed Rev. Messrs. L. W. BANCROFT, W. NEWTON, and A. M. MORRISON, a committee to prepare and submit a plan of operations. Also, on motion, the Rev. Mr. NEFF was appointed a committee to inquire on what terms property in the neighborhood, adapted for the present purpose of occupancy, could be obtained. Adjourned to meet at Bishop BEDELL's call.

A. M. MORRISON, *Secretary.*

GAMBIER, May 30th, 1864.

" An adjourned meeting called by Bishop BEDELL was held this morning in Rev. L. W. BANCROFT's room in Bexley Hall. Present, Right Rev. CHARLES P. McILVAINE, Bishop of the Diocese of Ohio; Right Rev. G. T. BEDELL, Assistant Bishop of the Diocese of Ohio, Rev. Messrs. NEWTON, BANCROFT, BLAKE, NEFF, TULLIDGE, MORRISON, President SHORT, and also the Rev. GEO. D. MILES of Wilkes Barre, Pa., and W. H. ASPINWALL, Esq., of New York. The following Report was presented, and after discussion adopted:—

" Inasmuch as the time has come when the successful prosecution of the work of Missions demands the establishment of a Missionary Training School, and inasmuch as our beloved brother Rev. J. G. AUER, has expressed his willingness to organize such a school, and to carry it on for the space of one year or more, therefore it is resolved by the Brethren in Christ here assembled, to establish such a school in Gambier, to be called the *Episcopal Missionary Training School* at Gambier, Ohio. Your committee would suggest the immediate appointment of a Board of Advice, and of a Board of Finance: The Board of Advice to consist of the Bishop of Ohio, *ex-officio,*—the Right Rev. G. T. BEDELL, D. D.,—the Rector of Harcourt Parish, Gambier, Ohio, *ex-officio*, the Rev. Prof. J. J. McELHINNEY, D. D., and the Rev. Prof. L.

W. BANCROFT. The Board of Finance to consist of the Rev. ALFRED BLAKE, Rev. PETER NEFF, JR., Rev. A. M. MORRISON, and the President of Kenyon College, *ex-officio*,—Rev. PETER NEFF, JR., acting as Secretary and Treasurer, each Board having power to fill vacancies, and the action of the Board of Finance in purchase and investment being conditioned on the approval of the Board of Advice. The committee would also suggest that Mr. AUER, be invited to enter upon his work in September next; the Board pledging his support, and that of the students who may be placed under his charge for the space of four years, believing that He who hears and answers prayer, will help them to meet every exigency and to supply every want."

Signed,   Rev. L. W. BANCROFT,
          Rev. WM. NEWTON,   } *Committee.*
          Rev. A. M. MORRISON.

It was also resolved to request the Board of Trustees of the Theological Seminary of the Diocese of Ohio, to set aside some of the College land for the future use and occupancy of the Missionary Training School. Bishop BEDELL gave a pledge of five hundred dollars towards the erection of a building. Bishop McILVAINE, said that " now having launched this noble enterprise, we will pray for God's blessing upon it," and, with a fervent prayer for the success of this new gospel enterprise by Bishop McILVAINE, the meeting was solemnly closed.

PETER NEFF, JR., *Secretary.*

1864.—June 1st.

The Rev. Mr. AUER visited Gambier, and before a meeting which had been convened, he presented written plans and designs for the school, and explained them at length. Soon after, with a view of opening the Missionary Training School in the fall, the house and land of THOMAS BIRD, M.D., of Covington, Kentucky, situated on the Amity road, North of Bexley Hall was leased at an annual rent of about $90. After a few alterations should be made it was believed the property would answer well for the beginning and experiment of the school. Mrs. BEDELL assumed the payment of the rent so long as it should be used for this Missionary purpose; the support of the Principal was provided by a member of Christ Church, Germantown, Pa. WM. H. ASPINWALL, Esq., made a donation of $500 for contingent expenses; and other contributions were soon after received.

1864.—July 3.

The Board of Advice was altered so as to comprise the members of the Theological Seminary of the Diocese of Ohio, *ex-officio*.

CHANGE OF NAME TO GAMBIER MISSION HOUSE.

The Institution began to be popularly known by the name of "*The Gambier Mission House,*" although this substitute was not adopted, by formal vote of the Boards, until December 17th, 1864, when it was adopted in place of the former title of "*The Episcopal Missionary Training School.*"

1864.—October 6.

The following resolution commendatory of the institution was adopted by the Board of Missions of the Protestant Episcopal Church in the United States of America, at their annual meeting held in Cleaveland, Ohio;—

"On motion of the Rev. Dr. CLARKSON:

"*Resolved*, That this Board concurs with satisfaction, and gratification in the endorsement of the *Gambier Mission House* by the committee on the Foreign Report, and it heartily approves of the establishment of such Missionary School, and anticipates with confidence, happy and blessed results from the planting of such an institution in our midst; and the Board earnestly recommends the Gambier Mission House to the sympathy and generosity of the Church in general."

The Mission House was opened on September 1st, 1864,[*] with *one* student. Three others, and a young native African, came during September and October, and also three German clergymen in this country (all of them educated at Basle). One of these (Rev. W. C. DUERR) was sent to Africa, and another (Rev. A. C. HŒHING,) to China, by the Foreign Committee.

MISSION HOUSE INAUGURATION.

1864.—Thursday, October 14th.

"The services arranged for the more formal inauguration of this deeply interesting and hopeful enterprise,

---

[*] NOTE.—Allusion to this meeting is made in a letter of the Rev. E. W. SYLE, Missionary in China, written at Shanghae, March 19th, 1869.

" * * * * * * The Mission House struggled into existence in spite of much indifference, distrust, and almost disdain on the part of those who should have welcomed and cherished it; and I see in this a token of its being a plant of our Heavenly Father's planting; for the worldly-minded made it the object of their enmity, and the worldy wise distinguished it by their distrust.

I well remember the meeting, (and so will Brother MORRISON,) when five of us inaugurated its commencement by uniting in a prayer for God's blessing upon it. The opening exercises had been announced long beforehand in the papers, and I had travelled from Pelham, New York, to Gambier, to be present at them. But *five* were all that came—AUER, DUDLEY SMITH, ARCHIE MORRISON, and his wife, in whose parlor, in the evening of the day, and after the failure of all appearance of interest on the part of others, we five (as I mentioned before) committed the infant Institution to the nursing care of the God and Father of us all."

(postponed on account of the absence, in Cleveland, of some appointed to take part in them,) were held this evening in Ross Chapel, Bishop BEDELL presiding. The Missionary Prayers set forth for such occsasions by Bishop McILVAINE, were offered. The Rev. WILLIAM NEWTON made a brief address on the origin, nature, and true scope of the Missionary spirit and work. The students of the Mission House, led by Mr. AUER, then sang the following, which is a translation, by himself, of one of the hymns of the Parent House at Basle:—

> WITH the Lord thy work begin!
> Trust in Him alone, and ever,
> Nothing in thy strength endeavor,
> Lowly hearts His favor gain:
> With the Lord thy work begin!
>
> With the Lord thy work begin,
> Then the prize seen at a distance,
> Shall be gained. Through His assistance,
> Thou art sure the prize to win:
> With the Lord thy work begin!
>
> With the Lord thy work begin!
> Strength and courage—He will send it;
> And thy work—with joy thou 'lt end it,
> If He its first and last has been:
> With the Lord thy work begin!

At the Bishop's call the Rev. Principal of the Mission, Mr. AUER, gave a sketch of the steps which led to its establishment, he dwelt upon the various distinguishing characteristics of the school, and pointed out those elements of mission-work on a pagan field, which call for the establishment of just such a department of special Missionary preparation. He urged that in order to communicate those special practical aptnesses, and that peculiar quality, whether of acquirement or training, which alone, humanly speaking, can ensure that *the Missionary shall be well furnished for his work, before he enters upon it,* and so shall have the best prospect of happiness and usefulness *in* it, such a school is altogether indispensable.

The Mission House students led, as before, by their Principal, then sang the following hymn, also translated from one of those in use at the Basle school:—

 I.—Our work is Thine, Lord Jesus Christ,
  We follow Thy command,
  And as Thy work, most highly prized,
  It shall forever stand.
  But, ere the grain of wheat we sow,
  Its growth and fruitfulness can show,
  It has beneath the ground to be,
  Must get from its own body free:—
   Through death made free;
   From its old nature free.

 II.—Thou Jesus Christ, our Head and Lord,
  Through sufferings went'st to God,
  And leadest who believe Thy work,
  With Thee, the self-same road,
  Let then, O Lord, all that are here,
  Thy sufferings and Thy kingdom share,
  Through Thy death's door, from death and night,
  Exalt us to Thy Heavenly light:—
   Through night to light;
   Through night to Heavenly light.

Rev. Dr. HALLAM, of New London, Conn., who was present as the only representative of the Board of Missions, gave a brief and feeling address of cheer and God's-speed, on the part of the Board, and of the Church at the East, whom he was sure he might assume to represent, on this occassion, without risk. Bishop BEDELL followed Dr. HALLAM, thanking him cordially for the lively interest in the Mission House which had brought him to the spot to see it, and for the earnest good-wishes he had expressed in its behalf. He felt sure from what he himself had seen and heard, that the Dr. had not exaggerated the interest felt, and the approval expressed in other quarters of the Church, while, with regard to the Board of Missions, he had been even surprised at the unanimity and cordiality, with which, at their recent session, they had endorsed the principle on which it was founded, and the plan on which it was to be conducted. He proceeded to administer a rebuke to the too common sentimentalism which prevailed on such occassions, and which contented itself with enjoying the good things provided for the hearer, and expressing its satisfaction with the " good meeting" and then rested, feeling its duty quite discharged. While he knew there were many who would give as God had prospered them, and many more who would pray, he wanted to suggest a simple, very practical, and highly useful method, open to every one present, and which he urged them to put in practice before they courted their pillows for the night,—and that was to *write at least one letter* to some Christian friend, most likely to take a practical interest in the matter, introducing the Mission House to their notice, and urging its value and its necessities.

A collection was taken amounting to $183.95, well distributed, after which the services closed with the Missionary hymn and prayer.

Thus the Mission House was fairly and formally launched. The number of inmates soon increased beyond the capacity of the building temporarily occupied. During the first year a neighbor did the washing and cooking at the Mission House, the Principal acting also as housekeeper. After that the students ate in a boarding-house, and most of them used the unoccupied rooms in Bexley Hall, which were kindly offered by the Seminary authorities. Mr. AUER was greatly assisted in his secular duties by the Treasurer, PETER NEFF, Esq., and other friends at Gambier. Mrs. NEFF, assisted by a special sewing society of the Gambier ladies, took care of the laundry troubles. President SHORT, of Kenyon College, Prof. STONE, Rev. A. M. MORRISON, and four students of the Seminary, did the teaching during several months which Mr. AUER spent in the East, in order to raise funds for a new building. He has taken occasion to record his thanks to all the helpers and sympathizers, at that time, and adds, that "under God, most of the success of the Mission House, is chiefly due to the unabating sympathy and most valuable assistance of Bishop BEDELL."

PLANS FOR THE NEW SITE AND BUILDING, AT GAMBIER.

1865.

The necessity of better accommodations was more and more felt, and in the summer of 1865, plans were laid for the erection of a new building. The Trustees of the Gambier Seminary and College granted to the Mission House a large tract of land on the Bishop's Hill, forming an eligible site for the new Mission House.* It was an elevated position, commanding a magnificent view of the Kokosing Valley. On Thursday, September 28th, 1865, ground was broken for the new building, and as about $1,800 were in hand, sufficient to finish the basement, it was resolved, notwithstanding the lateness of the season to proceed with the work so far as the funds in hand would carry it on. The total proposed cost of the building was $15,000. It was to be of stone finished off with brick. The work however, was very soon stopped by the frost, and the very important change which we shall next notice, led to the final abandonment of the work upon this building.

---

* Note.—The following are the boundaries of the tract granted to the Mission House, viz:—

The College land lying North of the Bishop's residence and more particularly described, as follows:—Beginning at the N. W. corner of Bishop Bedell's lot where it intersects Mrs. M. T. C. Wing's line, thence North on said Wing's line to a point where the South line of a Street running E. and W. and lying North of and on Mr. E. C. Benson's North line, would intersect, thence East on said South line of said Street continued, to the N. W. corner of Mr. M. White's lot, thence South on the West line of Mr. White's and Rev. A. Blake's line to where the Bishop's North line intersects the said West line, thence West along the Bishop's North line to place of beginning:—Containing twenty acres more or less.

REMOVAL OF THE MISSION HOUSE TO PHILADELPHIA.
1866.

"This movement really originated, (though at that time it had no connection with the Gambier Mission House, which had not then been thought of,) in the purpose of the late Bishop POTTER, of Pennsylvania, to associate with the Philadelphia Divinity School, which it was one of the latest labors of his life to found and foster, a distinct Missionary department. It may be said that this movement really originated in that purpose; for, though Bishop POTTER's idea took a very different shape from that which has now, under Providence, developed itself into the Mission House, yet it was this purpose on his part which first led the Rev. Mr. AUER to propose to certain earnest and interested brethren in Philadelphia, the foundation of a distinct and independent institution for such work. Providential circumstances, (already alluded to,) prevented at that time the consummation of Mr. AUER's plan in Philadelphia, and when, a few weeks subsequently, (June 18, 19, 20, and 21st, 1864,) the idea of such an institution was sketched out by him in a course of Missionary lectures to the Theological Students and others in Bexley Hall, Gambier; three gentlemen, who were there present, at once took it up and pressed the matter to its issue in the establishment of the institution, shortly thereafter, at that place.

Some time after Bishop POTTER's sad and sudden death, (July 4, 1865,) his successor, Bishop STEVENS, who had never ceased to desire the carrying out, in some shape, of the idea of a Missionary institution, or department, in connection with the Divinity School in Philadelphia, began to move in the direction of some sort of negotiation in reference to the Mission House. Indeed, as early as during the session of the Triennial General Convention, held in Philadelphia in October, 1865, the matter was talked over between himself and the Bishop and Assistant Bishop of Ohio, but nothing definite was determined at that time.

Bishop STEVENS, however, was deeply interested, and convinced that there were very strong reasons why the Institution would exercise a more direct and central influence, and make itself more felt as a power in the Missionary system of our Church, if located in Philadelphia, in place of Gambier. Under this conviction, Bishop STEVENS was led to seek some definite movement in the direction indicated, and one of the last things he did before sailing for Europe, February 20th, 1866, under the imperative commands of his physicians, was to call a meeting of a number of clergy and laymen, requesting them to take charge of an effort to transfer the Gambier Mission House to Philadelphia. It was one of his last administrative acts ere leaving home, and was performed in the midst of much weakness and pain. A request thus emphasized was not left neglected, and the persons thus called together at this meeting in Philadelphia, at once instituted measures for the accomplishment of this result. The Rev. M. A. De Wolfe Howe, D.D., and Rev. Robert J. Parvin, and others, were appointed a committee to confer with the authorities at Gambier upon this topic. On February 8th, 1866, Mr. Parvin addressed a letter to Mr. Auer at Gambier on the subject, which after being considered by the Boards there, resulted in the appointment of Bishop McIlvaine, Rev. A. M. Morrison, and President Short, as a committee to confer with the Philadelphia committee.

The two committees were to have met and conferred during the sessions of the Delegate Meeting of the Board of Missions at Detroit, in February. Unavoidable obstacles prevented the full accomplishment of this purpose, and consequently the Rev. Mr. Parvin returned from Detroit with the Gambier committee, and enjoyed the opportunity of a full conference with the Mission House Board there, and of a personal inspection of the ground. This visit led to the following correspondence, which will explain more adequately than we could otherwise do, the grounds upon which, after a most deliberate and careful consideration, the important step of the removal of the Institution was determined upon.

CHELTEN HILLS, PA., March 13th, 1866.

DEAR BISHOP BEDELL:—Our Mission House Committee met last evening and listened to the Report which I had to make to them, as to the views, feeling, &c., of your committee, and as to the present condition of affairs in regard to your proposed new building, * * * * * * * I believe that I gave to our committee a true account of the case, and I know that I assured them of the kind and good feeling of all of you, and of your good desires for the Mission House, independently of the question of location, whilst I further expressed your intentions to go on heartily with the work at Gambier, unless we could show good and satisfactory reasons for a removal. I submitted neither resolution, nor suggestion looking to one. The whole question was then fairly considered, and the result was an unanimously adopted resolution, requesting Dr. HOWE and myself to address a letter to your committee, proposing the transfer of the Mission House to the city of Philadelphia, or its immediate vicinity, and setting forth the reasons on which we present the request. * *

Sincerely and Respectfully Yours,

ROBERT J. PARVIN.

PHILADELPHIA, March 15th, 1866.

To the Trustees or Managers of the
Mission House, at Gambier:

DEAR BRETHREN:—In the conference which you lately afforded a member of this committee, it was made to appear desirable that some more formal statement of reasons should be given by the friends of the enterprise in this city, why, in their judgment, the interests of the Mission House, and of the cause to which it is auxiliary, would be promoted by its removal to this vicinity.

The committee who, through the undersigned, have signified to you their readiness to provide for the support of the school, if transferred, have charged us to lay before you the considerations which have influenced them to propose its removal. We need not say that they are affected by no spirit of rivalry, or even indifference to the noble Church Institutions at Gambier. On the contrary, all whom we represent regard them with the liveliest interest, and wish them full prosperity. Neither are we actuated by any desire to deck our own Divinity School with new attractions and honors. We are consciously moved only by a desire that the Mission House shall be made instrumental of the greatest amount of good, by having the best facilities for doing its appropriate work.

We respectfully submit to you the following reasons :—

1st. The Mission House would, in this region, be in the midst of a much larger Church population. The Church community in and about this city is a very large and influential element. It is likely, therefore, to furnish more material out of which Missionaries are to be made.

2d. It is not natural for such to think of going six or eight hundred miles into the interior for their training. Nor is a school so far removed from their observation likely to suggest the thought of Missionary service to those who might otherwise be moved to engage in it.

3d. Foreign Missionary wants and duties are most likely to present themselves to the minds and consciences of those who live near the sea-board, and whose business and other associations are with foreign countries.

4th. In the Atlantic States the need of Home Missionaries is not so urgent as in the great West, and therefore the hearts of men who here desire to consecrate their lives to the spread of the gospel, are more free to entertain the claims of those who have never heard the Saviour's name.

5th. If there be not greater wealth in the Eastern than in the Western cities, it has been longer possessed; and its possessors have been more habituated to its bestowal on religious and charitable objects. If the Mission House, which now has little more than a name to live, is to grow to adequate or effective proportions, it must be supplied with much larger resources. Whence can they be drawn? From the East or the West? And will they flow as freely from this region, if the centre of operations be far off?

6th. It is conceded that it is very desirable that Foreign Missionaries should have some knowledge of the healing art. No place in the country offers such facilities for medical education as Philadelphia. Mission pupils could doubtless attend the lectures at our Medical Colleges gratuitously.

7th. When Foreign Missionaries return statedly to this country for recruit, they usually pass much of their time in our larger Atlantic cities, for the purpose of visiting the churches, and becoming acquainted with the friends of Missions, on whom they are most largely dependent. How convenient it would be for them, and what an advantage to the inmates of the House, if they could find a temporary home at the Mission School; and either in social converse, or occasional lectures, give the embryo Missionaries some practical ideas of the life which is before them; and get acquainted with their future associates.

8th. We submit, finally, that it would be an advantage to have the Mission House not far from the committee who have in charge the Foreign Department of the Church's Missions. Two members of that committee reside in Philadelphia. Some personal knowledge of candidates for the Foreign fields might protect the committee from the costly mistakes into which they sometimes fall by sending incompetent persons, or good persons to the wrong stations.

We might multiply reasons yet further, but to us these seem cogent and sufficient.

If you accept them as convincing we shall be ready to provide temporary accommodations for the school whenever you are ready to transfer it, and to make all reasonable arrangements for receiving the assets of the Institution, and putting it in operation here, with resources undiminished by the fact of transfer.

Commending the whole subject to your prayerful consideration, we remain, dear brethren, very truly and respectfully yours,

M. A. DE WOLFE HOWE,
ROBERT J. PARVIN.

GAMBIER, OHIO, March 23d, 1866.

REV. AND DEAR BRETHREN:—

We have been requested by the Board of the Gambier Mission House to respond to your communication of March 15th, received last evening, proposing the removal of the "House" to the neighborhood of Philadelphia. We desire to write in an equally frank and fraternal spirit.

The reasons for removal urged in your letter certainly possess weight. On the other hand, we must take into consideration the advantages afforded to the Mission students by the proximity of these several Church Institutions, viz., a Grammar School, a College, and a Theological Seminary. These combine to furnish them instruction in whatever branches they may be found deficient, as well as to prepare them for the ministry. We are not aware that these advantages can be so *readily* obtained elsewhere; nor can they be obtained at any other point from Institutions strictly Episcopal.

We must take into consideration also the advantages arising from the wholesome retirement of Gambier; from its peculiar salubrity; from the comparative economy of living; from the freedom from temptations incident to city life, and especially those which lead candidates for the ministry to prefer settled parochial cures to the Missionary work. We have regarded also as important the healthful spiritual influence, which, by God's blessing, pervades the Hill.

Yet we cannot be insensible to the especial force of a consideration suggested by yourselves, viz: the possibility that a larger Missionary interest may be concentrated by its location at the East, and a greater efficiency given by an increased pecuniary support. So far, we have experienced no difficulty on this latter point. The Lord has graciously and fully sustained our effort for the initiation and due development (thus far) of our plan. Yet, for its proper enlargement, it needs a great increase of contributions in future years. We concede that you have better opportunities than we, for judging as to the increase of Missionary interest which will be gained by removing the "House." If the Foreign Committee should express a wish in the premises, or if we could be assured that the removal would secure their hearty co-operation in the plan, it would go far towards directing our decision.

On another point we are solicitous, in case the removal be determined upon, viz., that the characteristic features of the plan, as already announced, should be faithfully preserved ; and that the name " Mission House " should be retained. Many of those who have contributed to this object desire that it shall *not be a training-school*, understanding by that term something less than *education ;* and believing that our Missions need ministers completely educated.

The feature of a Missionary Home for returned and disabled Missionaries is very dear to us.

On another point explicitness is desirable. Certain sums have been contributed for the erection of a permanent building. As Trustees, we feel bound to secure the devotion of all such sums to that purpose; and if the " House " shall be removed, we desire to transfer that fund intact. But we have expended a small portion of it in preparations for building, all of which will be rendered useless if we accept your proposal. We shall confidently look to you, therefore, to bear the expenses now alluded to, in order that we may transfer the said fund undiminished. It is our intention also, if the removal shall be decided on, to transfer to you all the available assets, viz., furniture, building-materials, full set of working-drawings, and the balance of the general fund. Meanwhile we have to-day suspended work upon the building, and await your reply to the several suggestions of this note, with which we shall hope to be favored at the earliest moment.

We have also laid this correspondence before the Bishop of this Diocese, whose judgment we do not feel at liberty to anticipate, and whose response we shall await.

You will unite with us in the earnest prayer that the Lord of the Harvest, will so direct both parties in this movement, that having no aim but His glory, His blessed cause may be the most abundantly advanced.

We remain yours respectfully and affectionately,

G. T. BEDELL,
A. M. MORRISON.

To Rev. Dr. HOWE,
    Rev. R. J. PARVIN. } *Committee.*

PHILADELPHIA, March 28th, 1866.

Right Rev. Sir and Rev. Brother:—We have your favor of the 25th inst., and have given serious consideration to its suggestions. We are not unaware that there are some advantages in the position of the Mission House at Gambier, which we cannot promise to match in this city, or its vicinity. " Retirement " is in some respects to be desired, in others to be deprecated. " Salubrity " we think we can promise hereabouts. In " economy of living " you could probably surpass us, though some necessary articles of consumption are more costly with you than with us. The larger expenditure for support which may be incurred here, will be of no consequence if the income be increased in equal measure. In wholesome spiritual influences, there may be here some compensation, for what would unquestionably be lost.

We are not able to speak with confidence of the course which the Foreign Committee might take if the Mission House were removed to the East. Most of the individuals composing that committee have spoken approvingly of the plan of its removal. So far as we know there would be no disposition on the part of the friends of the Institution to change its name, or materially to alter its character and course of instruction.

We have nowhere in or about Philadelphia, such a complete circle of Church Scholastic Institutions as crown the Hill at Gambier. But we do not apprehend that there would be any difficulty in securing for students, who may require help outside of the Mission House, instruction in any department, under proper auspices. We understood, before writing our former communication, that it would be expected of us, if the Institution were placed under our care, to replace in its endowment, or available means, whatever sums have been expended therefrom in preparing for it a permanent abode at Gambier. And we intended in that letter to express an assent to that idea, or proposal. We think it will be seen, on reference to our former letter, that we accept that obligation. At any rate, we do now explicitly agree to the proposition, concerning fiscal affairs, contained in your letter of the 23d, understanding that in a statement given by Mr. NEFF, the Treasurer, under date of February 24th, we have an approximate idea of what we should receive, and what it would devolve on us to pay, in case the transfer be made.

Praying that the Lord may in this and all things, direct and rule your hands and ours, we remain very truly and respectfully yours,

M. A. DE WOLFE HOWE,
ROBERT J. PARVIN.

To the Right Rev. Dr. BEDELL,
  The Rev. A. M. MORRSION.

TOLEDO, OHIO, April 5th, 1866.

DEAR BRETHREN:—The communication from Rev. Dr. HOWE, and Rev. Mr. PARVIN has been laid before Bishop McILVAINE, and we have consulted respecting it. We hereby assent to the removal of the Mission House; grateful to God that our Board have been privileged to initiate the scheme, and to carry it so far towards success, as to show to the Church its entire feasibility.

We unite in sincere prayers that God will bless it abundantly in the hands of our brethren of Philadelphia.

In behalf of the Bishop and for myself;
Yours affectionately,

G. T. BEDELL.

To the GAMBIER MISSION HOUSE BOARD.

1866.—April 11.

The last two of the above letters having been laid before the Mission House Board, at a meeting held at Gambier, April 11th, 1866, the following resolution was unanimously carried:—

"*Resolved*, That the proposition of the Committee in Philadelphia for the removal of the Gambier Mission House to that city be, and the same hereby is, accepted: that the Corresponding Secretary be instructed to communicate this action, and to signify the readiness of the Mission House Board to transfer the Institution so soon as it shall be learned that the necessary arrangements are sufficiently advanced in the new locality, and that the Treasurer be empowered to carry out all requisite measures for the disposal of the available assets in Gambier, and the transportation of such as it shall be found advisable to remove; and also to transfer to the party duly appointed to receive the same in Philadelphia, the balance of the Building Fund, with the Books, Plans, &c., &c."

Most of the material which had been collected for the foundation of the new buildings was advantageously disposed of, and the least possible loss incurred by the removal of the institution.

THE FAREWELL TO GAMBIER.

1866.—June 4th.

"A farewell meeting was held in Bexley Hall Chapel, at 9 o'clock, on Monday morning, June 4th, 1866. The members of the Board, the Rev. Mr. AUER and the nine Mission House students, and a number of friends of the Mission House, both gentlemen and ladies, were present. After appropriate religious services, addresses were made by Professors MCELHINNEY and GARDINER, Rev. Messrs. AUER and BLAKE, President SHORT, and a few words of simple farewell from other members of the Mission House Board present.

On the part of the Mission Students, a brief and most feeling response was given by Mr. BERNSTEIN, to the many and most sincere expressions of interest which were made by one and another during the course of the meeting, which was concluded by prayer from a member of the Mission Board, and a warm hand-shaking of farewell all round. It was pleasant to see taking part in this expression, with characteristic warmth, the good ladies of Gambier, who from the first, felt and manifested so true an appreciation of the Mission House; and in particular, the most estimable lady of the Treasurer, who unsolicited, charged herself with those constant maternal cares of the needle and the wardrobe, which are so invaluable to young men under the circumstances, and yet which any head of a household will know to be —especially in addition to her own home-cares of the same sort—no light undertaking.

Unanimous on the part of all present, were, unmistakably, the feelings of genuine regret in submitting to that slowly-reached judgment on the part of the Mission Board, which led to the transfer of the Institution, of lively thankfulness that to Gambier had been accorded the privilege at least to plant the seed, and to nurture it in its earliest germination; and of continued, prayerful interest in the work as it shall proceed from its new and permanent centre.

In responding to the expression of these sentiments, Mr. AUER took occasion, among other things, to announce his intention of reserving in the fine new Mission House building in Philadelphia, one guest-room,—which he should label GAMBIER,—for the accommodation of such friends from the Western cradle of the Institution, as might, from time to time, favor it with their friendly presence.

At the final meeting of the Mission House Board, held immediately after the close of the farewell services before they adjourned *sine die*, a committee was appointed consisting of President SHORT, Prof. GARDINER, and Rev. A. M. MORRISON, to draft the following resolutions appropriate to the occasion.

WHEREAS, After much prayerful deliberation and consultation, it has seemed best, on the whole, to yield to the wishes of the friends of the Mission House in Philadelphia, and to consent to its removal to that city, where it will be under their immediate care, now, therefore, in view of this important change, constituting an era in the history of an enterprise, which by God's blessing has been here nursed into a condition of much promise for its future growth and usefulness, and deeply feeling what has been expressed in the farewell services just held, be it *Resolved:*—

1*st.* That we recognise with devout gratitude to God the earnest and faithful labors of the Principal, the Rev. J. G. AUER, to whose untiring exertions the beginning and present prosperity of the Mission House is due; and we ask for him God's further abundant blessing, both in the immediate establishment of the Mission House in its new home, and afterwards in his own chosen work among the heathen of Africa.

2*d.* That we also implore the Divine blessing upon the Mission House itself, that the change which, on the whole, has seemed wisest and best to us, may be blessed from above; this Institution be so prospered as to become henceforth an important aid in the great work of evangelizing the nations; and the Divine Spirit be so poured out upon its members, now and hereafter, that they and their work may be recognized to the praise and glory of His name.

3*d.* That while we ourselves part with this Institution with the deepest regret, we very earnestly commend it, especially in these days of its infancy, and at this critical period of its removal, to the interest, care, and prayers of our brethren in Philadelphia, assuring them that *our own interest*, labors, and prayers shall be with them, and that "The Gambier Mission House" will ever be dear to us and remembered by us before the Throne of Grace.

1866.—June 5.

On the next day, Tuesday, June 5th, Mr. AUER left Gambier with eight of the students attached to the Mission School, and on arriving at Philadelphia the next day, they went at once to the newly acquired building. He left one student behind him at Gambier, and directed two others who were waiting for admission to report immediately at Philadelphia.

Thus the transfer was accomplished, and the Mission House exercises began in Philadelphia with one Principal and ten students.

THE WELCOME TO PHILADELPHIA.

1866.—

The friends of this enterprise in Philadelphia, to whom Bishop STEVENS had entrusted the negotiation for the removal of the Mission House, had, after obtaining consent to the removal, entered into an agreement for the purchase of a suitable building for the school.

The title of the Institution was changed to that of "THE MISSION HOUSE OF THE PROTESTANT EPISCOPAL CHURCH IN THE UNITED STATES," and provision was made for a Board of thirty trustees, taken from different parts of the country.

The trustees were to choose officers to manage the affairs of the Institution, at the time of the Annual Commencement, on the fourth Wednesday in June; in the meantime, until the first meeting of the trustees, the following officers were appointed *pro tempore*:—

President—Right Rev. WM. BACON STEVENS, D. D., Bishop of Pennsylvania.

Vice President—Rev. M. A. DE WOLFE HOWE, D.D.

Cor: Secretary—Rev. RICHARD NEWTON, D. D.

Rec: Secretary—ANDREW WHEELER, Esq.

Treasurer—CHARLES B. DURBOROW, Esq.

With these the Rev. Messrs. R. C. MATLACK, J. W. CLAXTON, E. W. MAXCY, and D. O. KELLOGG, Jr., and Messrs. JAY COOKE, N. B. BROWNE, and B. G. GODFREY were associated, and a Committee of Finance, and a Committee on Discipline and Instruction were appointed.

A building was purchased for the Mission House in West Philadelphia, at the corner of Lancaster Avenue and Thirty-sixth Street. The mansion stood in the centre of a large lot, 120 feet wide and 190 feet deep, having shade trees, and several out buildings about it. The house contained seventeen or eighteen large rooms, the building being fifty feet square, and furnished excellent accommodations for lecture and recitation rooms. The location is excellent. It is in one of the most pleasant and healthy suburbs of the city, about half a mile from Market Street Bridge, and but six squares from the Philadelphia Divinity School. This affords the greatly desired facility of bringing these two

Church Institutions into daily communication with each other, and students in either one of the Houses can avail themselves of the advantages of the other, as may seem desirable.

The cost of the building and grounds was $17,000, and several thousand dollars were expended to put it into complete repair, and fit it for its new uses by the time the first students should arrive. JAY COOKE, Esq. contributed $10,000 towards the funds, and this princely donation has been succeeded by repeated, generous contributions from the same source for the support of the Mission House. Other donations were received, and in due time the Treasurer of the Gambier Mission House forwarded the sum of $2,476.98, being the amount received there for building purposes.

OPENING OF THE MISSION HOUSE IN PHILADELPHIA.

1866.—June 13.

The opening of the Mission House, at Philadelphia, was celebrated this day at 1 o'clock, P. M., by a meeting of a number of its friends, in the spacious lecture-room of the new house. As the Mission House is meant to be also a temporary home for invalid Missionaries, it was glad to open its door to welcome, first and so soon, the senior of the Missionary band. Bishop PAYNE who had arrived at New York from Africa, on the Saturday before, came on with his lady, to be a guest at the Mission House for a week. He presided at the services on this occasion, and after Mr. AUER had given a sketch of the history of the effort, the Bishop made an address expressing his delight and surprise, and thanking God with all his heart for what he saw and heard. Rev. Drs. NEWTON, BUTLER, and CLAXTON, and Rev. Messrs. J. GORDON MAXWELL, and A. B. ATKINS also spoke, expressing their interest and sympathy, and pledging their support. Bishop SMITH of Kentucky, who, passing through the city, had stopped to attend this meeting, came in before the close of the exercises and expressed his delight to see such a school of the church.

1866.—Wednesday, June 20th.

This evening, in the Church of the Epiphany, Philadelphia, a second meeting was held to welcome and introduce the Mission House. Addresses were made by Bishops PAYNE, and LEE, of Del., Rev. Drs. NEWTON and HOWE, and Rev. Mr. AUER. The attendance of the clergy was very large, representing most of the leading congregations of the city and vicinity, and one after another arose, in response to Mr. AUER's appeal, and assumed the support of one or more Scholarships, as well as the complete furnishing of the Mission House. The Church of the Epiphany led off with two Scholarships, and was followed by a dozen or more of the other churches, thus securing an immediate success for the enterprise.

THE FIRST BOARD.

1866.—June 27th.

On Commencement-day the following named persons became the Officers of the Mission House.

President.
RIGHT REV. WM. BACON STEVENS, D.D.,
Bishop of the Diocese of Pennsylvania.

Vice-President.
REV. M. A. DE WOLFE HOWE, D.D.

Corresponding Secretary.
REV. RICHARD NEWTON, D.D.

Recording Secretary.
ANDREW WHEELER, ESQ.

Treasurer.
CHARLES B. DUBORROW, ESQ.

Trustees.

Revs. M. A. DeWolfe Howe, D.D., R. Newton, D.D., W. Suddards, D.D., R. J. Parvin, R. C. Matlack, J. W. Claxton, Philadelphia; Rev. E. W. Maxcy, Bridgeport, Conn.; Rev. A. B. Atkins, Germantown, Pa.; Rev. D. O. Kellogg, Jr., Providence, R. I.; Rev. A. M. Morrison, Philadelphia; F. S. Winston, Esq., New York; Jay Cooke, Esq., Lemuel Coffin, Esq., John Bohlen, Esq., Philadelphia; Charles Spencer, Esq., Germantown, Pa.; B. G. Godfrey, Esq., Andrew Wheeler, Esq.,

C. B. Durborow, Esq., W. Welsh, Esq., T. H. Powers, Esq., N. B. Browne, Esq., C. P. B. Jefferies, Esq., Charles Riley, Esq., Philadelphia; F. R. Brunot, Esq., Pittsburg, Pa.; Russell Sturges, Esq., Boston.

Board of Managers.

Rev. J. W. Claxton, Rev. R. C. Matlack, Rev. A. B. Atkins, Rev. R. J. Parvin, N. B. Browne, Esq., C. P. B. Jefferies, Esq., Jay Cooke, Esq.

THE MISSION HOUSE HOISTS ITS FLAG.

1866.—Thursday, September 20th.

This afternoon the Sunday School of the Church of the Nativity, with some friends of the Institution, assembled in the lecture-room of the Mission House. This Sunday School had furnished a large flag and pole for the Mission House. Appropriate addresses were made by Rev. ROBERT C. MATLACK, Rector of the Church of the Nativity, Rev. Mr. AUER, Rev. Mr. PARVIN, Rev. Mr. MAXWELL, and Mr. THACHER. The flag is large, white, with four stars in the corners, and a red cross in the centre, surrounded by the words "FOREIGN MISSIONS." The cross represents the central point of Missionary life and preaching. The stars indicate the light going to the four corners of the earth. The sentiment of the occasion was admirably expressed in the following hymns written by teachers of the school, sung during the service:—

Lord, in Thy name we gather here,—
'The Banner of the Cross' we raise;
In loving kindness now draw near,
Accept this tribute of our praise.

We thank Thee that Thy truth divine
Beams brightly o'er our favored land;
Dear Saviour, prosper each design,
To spread its light, at Thy command.

Oh, send Thy quickening Spirit down,
To bless this consecrated place!
And with Thy richest favors crown
Thy chosen messengers of grace.

May every heart with ardor glow,
The tidings of Thy cross to give;
To dying heathen bid them go,
And preach Thy Word—'Believe and live.'

The glorious gospel Thou hast given,
Send forth Thy heralds to proclaim,
Till every nation under Heaven,
Rejoice in our Immanuel's name.

The Banner of the cross we raise
To Thee, Almighty God of love,
And hearts and voices join to praise
The Lord of all the worlds above.

Oh, may our joyful anthems rise,
And may the flag, to-day unfurled—
Emblem of love that never dies,—
Soon wave in triumph o'er the world.

From Zion's tower, oh let the light
To earth's remotest nations shine,

Disperse the gloom of heathen night,
Illumine with Thy love divine.

And to these messengers of God,
Oh, be Thy Holy Spirit given,
That they to every land abroad,
May bear the living light of Heaven

O'er India's plain, o'er Afric's sand,
Uplift the standard of our God;
Obedient to His great command,
"Go preach the Gospel of the Lord."

Till every people shall confess,
And echo back in joyful strain;—
Jesus, "the Lord our righteousness,"
Jesus, the Lord alone shall reign.

Lord, for this our happy meeting
Now accept our grateful praise,
Here thy grace and love repeating
We thy Gospel Banner raise.
    Aid us, Saviour,
To extend its cheering rays.

Helpless souls, in darkness lying,
Wait thy wondrous love to know;
Hark! the sound of voices crying
Save us, ere we sink in woe.
    Who will lead them
Where the living waters flow.

Oh, how dreary is the dwelling
Where thy name is never heard;
Where no song of praise is swelling,
Where thy love no heart hath stirred.
    Let us hasten
Forth to send thy precious word.

> Fired with zeal and expectation,
> Let thy servants onward press,
> Till each distant heathen nation
> Shall thy glorious name confess.
>   Hallelujah!
> Lord thou wilt our efforts bless.

After the services, the audience went into the garden, and the Mission students to the roof of the Mission House. The National Flag was first raised, and the students sang "*My Country 'tis of Thee.*" Then the white flag of the Mission House was hoisted, and the audience sang "*From Greenland's Icy Mountains.*" It sounded far and wide, people and carriages stopped, to look at the new phenomenon, and the neighbors evidently thought that the people in the house were the queerest that ever lived. Long may the students look on the Mission-flag, so white and peacefully waving. When streaming in the wind, its inscription will remind them of their destination, and its direction, no matter how it points, will always be away from their home, and towards the dark corners of the earth, the fields where they will contend for the cause of God and the Faith of Christ.

1866.

The Mission House began to fill rapidly. Mr. AUER says: "Sixteen students are here; next week I expect four more white men, and in two weeks four or five blacks from Hayti. Applications continue to come in, and I have not the heart to refuse them, although we are getting short of funds. Ten thousand dollars are still due on the house, furnishing, reparations and alterations, coal and stoves. Eating and living cost more than we counted for. But God is rich, very rich. The Library—which is also my office and recitation-room—is called 'GAMBIER.' The rooms in the second story have African names painted over every door; rooms in the third story have Asiatic and European names."

186.

Later in the fall Mr. AUER again in a letter to a friend, from which we make a few extracts, gives a vivid picture of the progress of the Mission House in Philadelphia.

"The Mission House is more than full. Yesterday, Mr. DUERR and family arrived with two gentlemen from Basle; one an old friend of mine, from the native place of Bishop GOBAT. He has been preaching in Brazil for ten years; now wants a place among the French in this country. The other is a candidate for our Church; was eight years teacher in Malta, one year in Alexandria, one year in London. I did not even know where to put all these people; but found a way (bath-room is too full for the present, until a visitor leaves.) Having given orders, I ran off to attend the operation on a sick friend, thinking they would be all in bed when I returned; whenever that might be. But I was mistaken; my own bed had to give a contribution first, and there was another young man with whom I had some correspondence; a proselyte from India, (Bombay;) lived long in Singapore, Canton, Hong Kong; educated in Hebron, half-converted in China, half in London, and here baptized. He is a good Hebrew scholar, very. The five Haytiens are here now, (seven colored men in all.) Mr. HINMAN, (Nebraska,) will send two Indians in a while. How we shall do without enlarging our borders, I know not; but such cares are none of my business. If all the world wants to be represented here, that *we* might be represented in all the world; let them come. We speak in the Mission House now:—English, French, Spanish, German, Danish, Polish, Hungarian, Arabic, Hindustanee, Zulu, Grebo, Ashantee, Accra, Hebrew, &c.

"Our funds are getting low. You ought to see how we eat. Expenses are running high. But I am not afraid. I was not at the Delegate Meetings, nor can I go to New York next week. Too much talking is no use, and I *must* work. The Lord will be our advocate."

1866.—Sunday, December 23d.

A largely attended meeting in behalf of the Mission House was held in St. Luke's Church, and addresses made by Bishop VAIL, of Kansas, Rev. Drs. HOWE and PRATT, and Rev. Mr. AUER.

1867.—October 17th.

At the annual meeting of the Board of Missions of the Protestant Episcopal Church, held in New York, the following resolution was offered by the Rev. WM. RUDDER, D. D., and passed *unanimously* :—

"*Resolved*, That in the MISSION HOUSE now established in Philadelphia, the Board recognize a valuable auxiliary to their work; and in the appointment of Mr. WARE,* one of its students, and his departure to the African field, a hopeful indication of the aid which may, in future, be more largely expected from that Institution, which they desire hereby to commend to the prayerful interest and the aid of all the faithful friends of Missions in our Church."

Hereby the Mission House was recognized as one of the General Institutions of the Church, and similar resolutions were passed at several succesive annual meetings of the American Missionary Society.

Mr. AUER'S RETURN TO AFRICA.

1867.—October 19th.

The Rev. Mr. AUER sailed this day for Africa, and on his arrival there on January 12th, 1868, he resumed his Missionary work with his characteristic energy and zeal. To some it might appear a pity that Mr. AUER should have returned, thus leaving the Mission House for the present without a *Missionary* among the staff of teachers.

---

* NOTE.—Mr. ROBERT G. WARE, went out from the Mission House in 1867. He was stationed at Cavalla, as Catechist, and afterwards at Cape Palmas. He died on August 31st, 1868, on board the steamship "Calabar," off the Gold Coast, as he was making a coast voyage to Accra to recruit his failing health. He was buried at Cape Coast Castle. Mrs. WARE stil remains engaged in Missionary labors at Cape Palmas.

But he said before he left:—"Most of the work can be done by any clergyman of the church, apt to teach; any one can make himself able to lecture on Missionary-work; and occasional visits from returned Missionaries, as well as regular correspondence with Missionaries in the field, cannot fail to keep the fire burning. The work is the Lord's, and needs no particular pillars to rest on. When a man knows the need of poor Africa,—and every letter from there is a sad cry for help,—it thrills through his heart like a trumpet-blast, and 'I must go as soon as I can,' is the response which he makes."

1868.—

We have traced the progress of the Mission House up to the close of 1868. The Rev. ALEXANDER SHIRAS succeeded Mr. AUER, as Principal; with the Rev. ARCHIBALD M. MORRISON as Instructor. The Rev. R. BETHELL CLAXTON, D. D., one of the Professors in the Divinity School, also assisted in the instruction of the Mission House students. About twenty students from different countries were in the Institution.

A few contributors had done all in their power towards the support of the Institution; but a mortgage of $10,000 still remained upon the Mission House Building, and the current receipts were hardly sufficient to meet the necessary expenses. The Board of Managers, therefore, at the instance of the President, Bishop STEVENS, effected an arrangement with Rev. SAMUEL DURBOROW, Rector of the Church of the Evangelists,

Philadelphia, to devote a few months to a special presentation of the claims of the Institution to the Church at large.

Rev. SAMUEL DURBOROW, Special Agent.—RESULTS.

1869.—January 17th.

The Rev. SAMUEL DURBOROW took a vacation of four months from his parochial work, and furnished with testimonials and appeals, visited Brooklyn, New York, Providence, Albany, Troy, Boston, Baltimore, Washington, Pittsburg, Cincinnati, Chicago, and many other places, as well as securing some liberal contributions in Philadelphia and vicinity. By his public addresses and from individuals, he secured in money and pledges about $17,000;—a sum sufficient to pay the mortgage on the Mission House, to settle all arrears, and defray its current expenses for some months. In addition to this, the Rectors of over thirty parishes, in various places, promised to make either parish or Sunday school contributions to the Mission House some time during the year, the amount of which could not be stated.

During his temporary agency, Mr. DURBOROW obtained from over one hundred of the most prominent bishops and clergy of the church, written commendations of the plan, object, organization, and location of the Institution. As valuable evidences of the general feeling entertained for the MISSION HOUSE, we introduce the following letters, *selected out of a much larger number expressing similar sentiments.*

EPISCOPAL ROOMS,
PHILADELPHIA, December 31, 1868.

REV. AND DEAR BROTHER:—I have just received from the Rev. Dr. HOWE, the letter appointing you as special agent to present the cause of the Mission House, at West Philadelphia, to the sympathy and support of the church at large. This appointment meets my cordial approval, and I do most earnestly request that you will accept it. In doing so, it will not be necessary that you should resign your parish, all that will be needed is to ask your Vestry to give you leave of absence for three or four months to enable you to visit the churches in Boston, Providence, New York, Baltimore, &c., and present the claims of the Mission House. During your absence the pulpit could easily be supplied, and many of your brethren would cheerfully contribute a service towards supplying the needed ministrations. The Mission House is, as you know, an institution of great importance, and may be made an instrument of immense value in spreading abroad the knowledge of the precious gospel of Christ. But its character is not known, and its claims have not been presented as they should be, and hence we may fail of success before even the experiment has been fairly tried.

In putting this agency in your hands, the committee and myself both feel convinced that you will, by God's blessing, awaken a new interest in its behalf—stir up the zeal of those now lukewarm or indifferent, and draw out the liberality of those who love our blessed Jesus.

Believing, therefore, that your parish will not suffer by your temporary withdrawal—that you yourself will be greatly benefitted in mind and heart, and body, by this new work, and that great good will redound to the Mission House, and the cause of Missions generally, by your accepting this appointment, I cannot too strongly urge you at once to accept and enter upon its important duties.

I remain, dear brother, very truly yours,

W. BACON STEVENS.

Rev. S. DURBOROW.

JANUARY, 1869.

"Having been present at the early meetings in Gambier, when the Rev. Mr. AUER suggested the plan of a 'MISSION HOUSE' for the United States, connected with the Protestant Episcopal Church,—like the one at Basle, Germany; and having ever since had a growing interest in the work, and a deepening sense of its importance, I thank the founders and present sustainers, in behalf of myself and congregation, for having given us an opportunity to contribute to this noble Mission work,— the foundation of all true church prosperity."

J. A. ASPINWALL,
Rector of Christ Church, Bay Ridge, Long Island.

BROOKLYN, L. I., January 17th, 1869

"Since 1865, when I first heard of the MISSION HOUSE, (then lately established,) from Rev. Mr. AUER, I have been heartily interested in it, and am persuaded that it will prove one of the most efficient of means for the success of Foreign Missions. I regret that the storm of this evening will prevent many of St. John's people from listening to the presentation of the subject, and the appeal by Rev. SAMUEL DURBOROW, and hope that any of them reading this, will add their gifts to the too scanty offerings in church."

ALEXANDER BURGESS,
Rector of St. John's Church, Brooklyn, Long Island.

JANUARY, 1869.

"I cordially commend the cause represented by the Rev. Mr. DURBOROW as one of the greatest excellence and importance:— our Church needs just such a MISSION HOUSE as that which is here presented to our kind people for their vigorous support."

HENRY E. MONTGOMERY,
Rector of the Church of the Incarnation, New York.

ST. ANN'S CHURCH, BROOKLYN HIGHTS,
January 22d, 1869.

"I have very great pleasure in giving my hearty endorsement to the 'MISSION HOUSE,' which is now specially represented by the Rev. Mr. DURBOROW. This Training School for the foreign field, I regard as of the first consequence. It is the foundation at once and the buttress of our great Missionary work in foreign lands. Just now the 'Mission House' is in need of assistance, and I can but feel that all who are made to understand the eminent importance of this most noble enterprise, will now come up to the help of the Lord."

NOAH H. SCHENCK,
Rector of St. Ann's Church, Brooklyn, Long Island.

JANUARY, 1869.

"I have felt great interest in the work of the 'MISSION HOUSE,' and have had intimate knowledge of its operations since its organization at Gambier, in 1864. I have recently visited the Institution in Philadelphia, and heartily commend it to the sympathies and liberal support of all who recognize the world as the field of Christian effort."

E. H. CANFIELD,
Rector of Christ Church, Brooklyn, Long Island.

JANUARY, 1869.

"While the command, 'Go ye into all the world and preach the gospel to every creature' remains upon the pages of our Bibles—we may be sure the MISSION HOUSE—which has been established expressly to aid in the fulfillment of that injunction—has the approval of our Blessed Master—and His approval must make it dear to our hearts."

W. T. SABINE,
Rector of the Church of the Atonement, New York.

FEBRUARY, 1869.

"I commend this noble work with all my heart, and shall contribute to it as largely as possible at Easter next."

WM. R. NICHOLSON,
Rector of St. Paul's Church, Boston, Massachusetts.

FEBRUARY, 1869.

"The undersigned cordially unites with his brethren in commending this noble Institution to all in the Protestant Episcopal Church, who believe in the duty and privilege of preaching the gospel to every creature."

FRANCIS M. WHITTLE,
Assistant Bishop of the Diocese of Virginia.

GAMBIER, OHIO, April 15th, 1869.

"From its inception in Gambier the plan of the MISSION HOUSE has had my hearty concurrence. Experience in its practical working has deepened the conviction of its value. I hope for the best results under its present management. It shall have my prayers, my influence, and my cordial co-operation."

G. T. BEDELL,
Assistant Bishop of the Diocese of Ohio.

PHILADELPHIA, January 28th, 1869.

"The MISSION HOUSE, West Philadelphia, should commend itself to every one desirous of seeing our Lord's Kingdom extended throughout the world. I feel a cordial interest in its work, and will do all in my power to aid it therein."

WM. RUDDER,
Rector of St. Stephen's Church, Philadelphia.

FRANKFORT, February 11th, 1869.

"I have for several years contributed the amount of a scholarship from the parish of which I am Rector, to the MISSION HOUSE. Such a scheme appears to me to be one of the most efficient modes of supporting Foreign Missions—a cause so distinctly commanded by the Lord Jesus, that the neglect of it may be the reason in the Divine counsels for the troubles in doctrine, &c., which have befallen our Church."

D. S. MILLER,
Rector of St. Mark's Church, Frankfort, Pennsylvania.

JANUARY 28th, 1869.

"I consider the MISSION HOUSE of the highest importance to the Missionary work of our Church. It was originated in my Diocese, and its removal to Philadelphia had my entire concurrence, and in its present position and needs, I urge upon our brethren its most cordial support."

CHARLES P. MCILVAINE,
Bishop of the Diocese of Ohio.

FEBRUARY, 1869.

"I concur with my brethren in expressing my interest in the MISSION HOUSE, and my cordial wishes for its prosperity."

J. JOHNS,
Bishop of the Diocese of Virginia.

NEW YORK, February 1, 1869.

"The difficult problem of Foreign Missions seems likely to find its happiest practical solution, as far as the obligations of our Church are concerned, in the wise and timely plan of the PHILADELPHIA MISSION HOUSE. I am very hopeful that it will awaken sympathies that have been too long dormant among us, and so bring back to the Protestant Episcopal Church blessings that will be withheld just so long as she is unfaithful to her most solemn obligation to preach her Master's gospel in 'the regions that are beyond.'"

HENRY C. POTTER,
Rector of Grace Church, New York.

PHILADELPHIA, February, 1866.

"I consider the MISSION HOUSE, West Philadelphia, one of the most interesting and important enterprises in which the Protestant Episcopal Church is engaged. It has had my most cordial sympathy from its very start. The present effort in its behalf has my heartiest endorsement.

RICHARD NEWTON,
Rector of the Church of the Epiphany, Philadelphia.

NEW YORK, February, 1869.

"The education of the Missionary, is that preliminary work, on which our Missionary cause must depend far more than we usually believe. We need for this field a special class,—more like the first Evangelists, and one which our common clerical training rarely furnishes. If this school can supply such a want, it will in a few years be the centre of a new Missionary-life amongst us."

E. A. WASHBURN,
Rector of Calvary Church, New York.

ELEVENTH AND CLINTON STREETS,
May 1st, 1869.

The MISSION HOUSE of the Protestant Episcopal Church is an Institution for training Missionaries for work among the heathen. Our Church is in *desperate need* of more men disposed and qualified for this work of faith and labor of love. The Mission House is the hope of the church. Let those who love this church sustain her school of the prophets and the Master will bless her and them for her sake.

M. A. DE WOLFE HOWE,
Rector of St. Luke's Church, Philadelphia.

NEW YORK CITY, February 6th, 1869.

"I am happy to express my hearty concurrence in the endorsement given by my brethren to the MISSION HOUSE in West Philadelphia. Such a school seems to be essential to the success of our Foreign Missions, and as providing for a suitable education for those who, not having had the benefit of a collegiate course, are desirous to give themselves to the work of Christ in the field of Foreign Missions, it meets a necessity which in no other way can be relieved. It deserves the cordial sympathy and liberal support of all who love Christ."

THOMAS H. VAIL,
Bishop of the Diocese of Kansas.

BOSTON, March 22d, 1869.

"It is hardly necessary for me to say that this Institution has my earnest support and desires for its cordial encouragement by others."

MANTON EASTBURN,
Bishop of the Diocese of Massachusetts.

FEBRUARY 9th, 1869.

"The MISSION HOUSE in Philadelphia is an instrumentality which seems to me indispensable to the future success of our Foreign Missions. I trust that its present wants will be met, and the means provided by the people of God for enlarging its usefulness."

A. N. LITTLEJOHN,
Bishop of Long Island.

MARCH, 1869.

"The PHILADELPHIA MISSION HOUSE has my hearty sympathy and good wishes, and I cheerfully commend it to those who desire the extension of the gospel, as a most important agency and help."

ALFRED LEE,
Bishop of the Diocese of Delaware.

NEW YORK, February 13th, 1869.

"The MISSION HOUSE in Philadelphia is an attempt to give persons designed for the Foreign Missionary work that special training and instruction so necessary for them. Similar attempts have been successfully made elsewhere, and I shall rejoice to know that this present effort is commending itself to the general sympathy and approval of our Church."

HORATIO POTTER,
Bishop of New York.

Signed also by   W. H. ODENHEIMER,
Bishop of New Jersey.

ALBANY, April 1st, A. D., 1869.

"The great practical advantage of the training which I believe the 'MISSION HOUSE' gives its students, to fit them for their foreign Missionary work, has always led me to feel much sympathy with its work, and great hopes of its successful establishment."

WM. CROSWELL DOANE,
Bishop of Albany.

PITTSBURG, April 12th, 1869.

"The MISSION HOUSE at Philadelphia, for the training of men for the foreign Missionary work of the church, has my heartiest commendation, as a wise and practical mode of preparing our Missionaries for their peculiar ministry in other lands. By it we secure a true economy of men and means. I trust that my Diocese will help forward every good agency of our foreign Missionary work."

J. B. KERFOOT,
Bishop of Pittsburg.

NEWARK, February 21st, 1869.

"I most cordially commend this MISSION HOUSE work, and will try to give it a lift the present year. The reflex influence of foreign Missionary interest in the Church, is an influence more to be desired than any other, for the development of earnest and enlarged views, and the true Apostolic spirit—the spirit of the Apostolic age."

MATSON MEIER SMITH,
Rector of Trinity Parish, Newark, New Jersey.

PROVIDENCE, March 10th, 1869.

"Having been connected with the MISSION HOUSE from the time of its removal to Philadelphia, my knowledge of its aims and affairs will justify me in cordially commending it to all the friends of foreign Missions in our Church. I look to its influence as the opening of a new era of energy and success under the Divine blessing, in the foreign field. Having done all I could for it in the past, I hope to persist in trying to win friends and support for it in the future."

D. O. KELLOGG, JR.,
Rector of Grace Church, Providence, Rhode Island.

PROVIDENCE, March 17th, 1869.

"It gives me great pleasure to commend the MISSION HOUSE at Philadelphia to the liberality of the members of St. John's. The cause of Foreign Missions, which has been so dear to them, will receive so great benefit from the Mission House that I feel sure they will give it their sympathy and support."

RICHARD B. DUANE,
Rector of St. John's Church, Providence, Rhode Island.

BOSTON, March 22d, 1869.

"I desire to express my entire and hearty concurrence with the above recommendations."

FRANCIS WHARTON,
Rector of St. Paul's Church, Brookline, Massachusetts.

NEW YORK, March 30th, 1869.

"I very cheerfully add my commendation of this object to those which have already been given."

JOHN COTTON SMITH,
Rector of the Church of the Ascension, New York.

TROY, April, 1869.

"I fully believe, that to make a man a proper Missionary, he should be educated as such."

T. W. COIT,
Rector of St. Paul's Church, Troy, Albany.

"I fully concur in the sentiment expressed above, by the Rector of St. Paul's, Troy; and would add the expression of my warmest sympathy in behalf of the effort being made to give it a practical embodiment in the MISSION HOUSE.

May the work be conducted in that spirit of wise discretion, and of large and loving toleration, which should characterise every undertaking of the Protestant Church Catholic."

E. N. POTTER,
Associate Rector of St. Paul's Church, Troy, Albany.

ALBANY, April, 1869.

"The 'MISSION HOUSE' deserves well of the Church. Its Managers have the confidence, as they should have the support, of all who desire the Church's growth. I heartily recommend it to the practical sympathy of the Church."

J. LIVINGSTON REESE,
Rector of St. Paul's Church, Albany.

BALTIMORE, April, 1869.

"During the Revolution, the combined armies of France, Russia and Hungary invaded Switzerland, and menaced the city of Basle. The citizens, escaping the horrors of Bombardment, showed their gratitude by erecting a MISSION HOUSE; a memorial of the past and prophetic of the future. May the Mission House of Philadelphia, sustained by Thank-offerings, prove a higher success in diffusing through all lands Apostolic Truth in Apostolic Order!"

GEORGE A. LEAKIN,
Rector of Trinity Church, Baltimore, Maryland.

BALTIMORE, April 5th, 1869.

"The MISSION HOUSE of the Protestant Episcopal Church in Philadelphia is known to me as one of the most noble Institutions in our Church. It was originated by Rev. Mr. AUER, a graduate of the Basle Mission House, in Switzerland, and now a Missionary of our Church in Africa. It has sixteen students on its roll, now preparing for foreign Missionary work. It depends for its maintenance entirely upon voluntary contributions. It is cordially commended to the generous patronage of the members of my church; and the mission of its Agent, Rev. Mr. DURBOROW, of the Church of the Evangelists, Philadelphia, is highly accredited by the authorities of the Institution, and its Right Rev. President."

JULIUS E. GRAMMER,
Rector of St. Peter's Church, Baltimore, Maryland.

GAMBIER, April, 1869.

"The MISSION HOUSE commends itself to my heartiest sympathy. The work it undertakes to accomplish—and has thus far accomplished with marked success—seems to me most important in its bearings upon the interests of our Church. I shall esteem it a pleasure, not less than an obligation, to aid the work in every way that lies in my power."

GEORGE A. STRONG,
Harcourt Parish, Gambier, Ohio.

CINCINNATI, April, 1869.

"I heartily endorse the cause presented by the Rev. Mr. Durborow, and I promise him help from my Sunday School."

JOHN H. ELLIOTT,
Rector of St. John's Church, Cincinnati, Ohio.

CHICAGO, April 26th, 1869.

"THE MISSION HOUSE is a noble Institution, and deserves the cordial support of the members of our Church throughout the land. It has the hearty sympathy of my parish."

H. N. POWERS,
Rector of St. John's Church, Chicago, Illinois.

THE MISSION HOUSE.

1869.

When the special pledges are paid into the Treasury the Institution will be free from debt and have secured to its sacred uses its building and grounds, which are estimated to be worth over $30,000. Having, however, as yet not one dollar as an endowment, it is dependent for its continued support on voluntary contributions. The trustees renew their appeal to the Church, especially to Christian men of means within it, for assistance. We incur no needless expenses. Our plans are all based upon principles of strict economy. We pay no high salaries, and sometimes our devoted Professors have waited long for their overdue stipends.

We trust, that very many whose attention has not hitherto been particularly called to the MISSION HOUSE, will begin, and continue to assist in its support. While no large endowment is asked, or deemed advisable, it is vitally important that provision should be made for regular payment of Instructors' salaries. Entrust us with a fund on which we may draw for the defrayment of moderate stipends, and you will set us free from painful perplexities.

The Institution *must* commend itself to all disciples who sincerely pray — "Thy Kingdom come!" The necessity for sending additional Missionaries to our Foreign Stations is absolute. Something must be done, or the startling question of abandoning the ground already won from heathenism will become imminent. That men can be obtained, and suitable men, any one who visits the Institution may satisfy himself. Christ's harvest-field it is, for which the laborers are preparing. Every workman is needed. Every hour is precious.

The general prospects of the MISSION HOUSE for the future are encouraging. The idea, the plan,—organization,—location,—object and necessity of it, all are abundantly approved. If the actual results produced from it have not yet been very evident or great, this is incidental and to be expected of an Institution so new in this country as the Mission House. The same was noticeable in those similar Institutions in other lands, which now are in successful operation, and are every year sending out a good supply of properly trained and educated men as Foreign Missionaries. There may be defects in the practical working of the Institution. Experience is showing where these are, and it is hoped that they may soon be remedied. Let those who are waiting for results be patient, hopeful and confiding; and, if properly sustained, the day is not far distant when the MISSION HOUSE IN PHILADELPHIA, will prove itself to all, one of the most useful Institutions of the Church, and one of the brightest ornaments of the Diocese in which it has been located,

OFFICERS OF THE MISSION HOUSE.

1868.—

President.
RIGHT REV. WM. BACON STEVENS, D.D.,
Bishop of the Diocese of Pennsylvania.

Vice-President.
REV. M. A. DE WOLFE HOWE, D.D.

Corresponding Secretary.
REV. RICHARD NEWTON, D.D.

Recording Secretary.
REV. ROBERT C. MATLACK.

Treasurer.
CHARLES B. DURBOROW, ESQ.
No. 234 Market Street.

Trustees.

Revs. M. A. DeWolfe Howe, D.D., R. Newton, D.D., W. Suddards, D.D., R. J. Parvin, R. C. Matlack, J. W. Claxton, Philadelphia; Rev. E. W. Maxcy, Bridgeport, Conn.; Rev. A. B. Atkins, Germantown, Pa.; Rev. D. O. Kellogg, Jr., Providence, R. I.; Rev. A. M. Morrison, Philadelphia; F. S. Winston, Esq., New York; Jay Cooke, Esq., Lemuel Coffin, Esq., John Bohlen, Esq., Philadelphia; Charles Spencer, Esq., Germantown, Pa.; B. G. Godfrey, Esq., Andrew Wheeler, Esq.,

C. B. Durborow, Esq., W. Welsh, Esq., T. H. Powers, Esq., N. B. Browne, Esq., F. R. Brunot, Esq., Pittsburg, Pa.; Russell Sturges, Esq., Boston; William L. Rehn, Esq., Philadelphia.

The Officers and the following Gentlemen compose the Board of Management.

Rev. J. W. Claxton, Rev. R. C. Matlack, Rev. A. B. Atkins, Rev. R. J. Parvin, N. B. Browne, Esq., Jay Cooke, Esq.

Instructors.

Rev. ALEXANDER SHIRAS, A. M., Principal,
Rev. Archibald M. Morrison, A. B.,
Rev. R. Bethell Claxton, D. D.

Instructor in Elocution.

PROF. E. M. EATON.

Medical Lecturers.

Harrison Allen, M. D., William Pepper, M. D.
Edward Rhoads, M. D., James Tyson, M. D.

Students

FOR THE SESSIONS OF 1868-9.

NAMES.	ENTERED.	CLASS.	BORN.	COUNTRY.	CHURCH CONNECTION.
A. Bernstein,*	Sept., 1865.	V.	1840	Austria.	Church of the Saviour, W. P.
W. H. Josephus,	" 1866.	IV.	1844	St. Croix, W. I.	Church of the Crucifixion.
Henry Meyer,	Ap., "	"	1844	Switzerland.	Church of the Saviour, W. P.
Gustav Purucker,	Oct., 1867.	"	1841	Germany.	" " "
Bertold Steiner,	" "	"	1844	England.	" " "
F. H. Stricker,	Sept., 1864.	"	1845	Germany.	St. Andrew's, W. P.
Fred. B. Whitney,	Nov. 1867.	"	1846	Canada.	Epiphany.
Chas. E. Benedict,	Oct., 1856.	III.	1849	Hayti, W. I.	Church of the Crucifixion.
Peter E. Jones,	" "	"	1848	" "	" " "
Wm. D. Kelly,	Sept., "	"	1844	U. States.	St. Thomas'.
Wm. L. Perrin,	Nov., 1867.	II.	1846	Canada.	St. Paul's.
Wm. H. Platt,	Oct., "	"	1844	U. States.	" " Cheltenham.
Zachary T. Savage,	Sept., "	"	1847	" "	Church of the Saviour, W. Phila.
Geo. C. Keenan,	" "	I.	1848	Ireland.	St. Paul's, Cheltenham.
John London,	" "	"	1844	England.	Church of the Saviour, W. Phila.
Chas. Mauny,	Feb., "	"	1850	France.	
Jos. W. Norwood,	Sep., 1868.	"	1843	N. Scotia.	Gloria Dei.
Ahsee Shearer.,	" "	"	1850	China.	Church of the Saviour, W. P.
John Waring,	Oct., 1866.	"	1850	Hayti, W. I.	Church of the Crucifixion.
Dan'l W. Hemans,	Ap., 1857.		1848	Dacota, Indian.	Church of the Saviour, W. Phila.
Luke C. Walker	May, "		1847	" "	Church of the Covenant.

* Left September 18th, 1868, to enter the General Theological Seminary, New York, and work among the Jews of New York City.

THE DESIGN OF THE MISSION HOUSE, is

1. To secure candidates for the foreign Missionary field.
2. To give them a satisfactory preparation for their work.
3. To test their fitness for it before sending them abroad.
4. To provide for invalid Missionaries a temporary resting-place, on their return to the United States.

In prime intent, it is an institution for educating Missionaries, and is essentially the same in plan with the English Church Missionary Institution, at Islington; St. Augustine's College, Canterbury; and the Mission House, at Basle, Switzerland. Like them, it grew out of the fact that our Theological Schools and Colleges have long failed to furnish a sufficiency of foreign Missionaries; and, like them, its special aim is to prepare fit laborers for the foreign fields under the care of the Protestant Episcopal Church in the United States. It affords to young men desirous to preach Christ among the heathen, an opportunity for a sound and useful education, embracing the most necessary parts of a college and seminary course, with certain elements of special preparation for their great life-work. Thus, it gives them, with their other studies, the essentials of medical knowledge, and teaching them particularly the diseases of the lands to which they are to go, instructs them how to guard against these, or how to remedy them, if incurred. It informs them, too, of the geography, the climate, the population, and the first elements of the languages of the fields in which they are to labor, that, when they reach these, they may be able to get early and intelligently at their work. And especially it endeavors to surround them, from the beginning to the end of their whole course, with such pure Christian influences as may keep freshly burning in them the flame of evangelical missionary zeal, and send them forth at last on their great enterprise, full of devoted love to Christ and the lost souls for whom he gave his life.

METHODS OF CONTRIBUTION.

I. Scholarships.—The smallest amount which can be named, for a student's support, is $300. Many Parish Rectors can secure from their congregations or Sunday Schools that sum, in annual contribution. Many others can assume a half-scholarship, by the yearly payment of $150. If desired by contributors, these foundations can be named, and thus be more definitely commended to the interest of their originators.

II. Collections.—The subject of Missions can be very practically presented to our churches, in connection with the Mission House. One of the Professors, or a Member of the Managing Board, will gladly accept any invitation to advocate the Mission House, within reasonable distance of Philadelphia.

III. Even if scholarships were obtained for every student in the Institution, a deficiency would still exist. We cannot venture to name a higher rate of support, but we earnestly solicit donations, in the way of substantial supplies. Books for the Library; provisions for the table; articles of furniture, bedding and clothing, for the young men, will prove exceedingly acceptable.

ADMISSION TO THE HOUSE.

The candidates desired are earnest Christian men, from seventeen to twenty-five years old, who feel that they are called to preach the Gospel to even the remotest nations of the earth. They must have, besides, a good English education, and at least the elements of Greek and Latin.

Each year a new class will be admitted, preference being given, amongst applicants, to those who present the best evidence of Christian character, advanced education, and adaptedness to missionary work. Men of superior acquirements enter at once the higher classes for which they are prepared.

Applications for admission should state distinctly the desire of the applicant to engage in missionary work abroad, and should be accompanied with a biographical sketch, (stating age, native country, education, occupation, and reasons for desiring to become a Missionary,) together with a testimonial from the pastor of his church, that he is of sound health, good mental capacity, and such earnest Christian spirit as will qualify him for usefulness in the missionary field. All should be addressed to " The Principal of the Prot. Ep. Mission House, W. Philad'a, Pa."

COURSE OF STUDIES.

The full curriculum, at the Mission House, embraces—

I. A PREPARATORY COURSE; consisting of the most essential parts of an Academic and Collegiate education.

II. A THEOLOGICAL COURSE; comprising such Theological studies as are needful for Missionary work.

It was originally intended that these courses should be each three years in length; but experience has shown that the second is liable to abbreviation, from the demands of the continually-growing field abroad: though, in all practicable cases, it is meant to keep it complete.

ACADEMIC AND COLLEGIATE COURSE.

FIRST YEAR.

Bible History (reading and reciting from the Bible itself).
English Grammar and Composition.
Geography.
Ancient History.
Arithmetic.
Latin Grammar and Reader.
Greek Grammar and Reader.
Singing and Music.

SECOND YEAR.

Sacred History of the Old and New Testaments (Kurtz).
Natural Philosophy and Astronomy.
Modern History.
History and Geography of Missions.
Algebra.
Latin (Cæsar).
Greek (Zenophon's Anabasis and Greek Test).
Rhetoric, and English Composition.
Drawing, Singing and Music.

THIRD YEAR.

Sacred History, continued.
History and Geography of Missions.
Greek Testament and Classics.
Latin Classics.
Geometry, Geology and Botany.
Rhetoric, Logic, Moral Philosophy, and Evidences of Christianity.
Elements of Medical Science.
Drawing, Singing and Music.

THEOLOGICAL COURSE.

FIRST YEAR.

Recitations and Lectures, with Junior and Middle Classes at the Divinity School, with others at the Mission House.

SECOND YEAR.

Recitations and Lectures, with Middle and Senior Classes at the Divinity School, with others at the Mission House.

THIRD YEAR.

Recitations with the Senior Class in the Divinity School.

Running through both these Courses will be—Instruction in the peculiarities of Missionary Lands; the Principles of Teaching (with illustrations in the practice of the Public Schools); and such parts of Medical Science as are likely to be most required.

CALENDAR.

Second Wednesday in September—School opens.
Thursday before Christmas—Examination and matriculation.
Second Thursday before Easter—Spring examination.
Third Monday in June—Annual examinations begin.
Fourth Wednesday in June—Commencement, and meeting of Trustees.

VACATIONS

Begin after the several examinations and the annual commencement in June.
Christmas Vacation ends January 2.
Easter Vacation ends Tuesday after Easter.
Summer Vacation ends second Tuesday in September.

RECEIPTS OF THE MISSION HOUSE, GAMBIER, OHIO,

From September 1, 1864, to June 1, 1866.

1864

W. H. Aspinwall, New York, for furniture	$500 00
S. B. Caldwell, " Scholarship	250 00
E. W. Dunham, " "	250 00
J. F. Sheafe, "	500 00
Jonas B. Kissam, "	10 00
J. H. Swift, "	20 00
Thos. Armstrong, "	40 00
Rob't Armstrong, "	20 00
W. B. Jackson, Utica, N. Y.	10 00
Admiral Dupont, Wilmington, Del.	500 00
Mrs. Susan K. Wade, Pittsburgh, Pa.	10 00
Judge Conyngham, Wilkesbarre, Pa.	25 00
Mrs. Jas. Bowman, Brownsville, Pa.	20 00
Rev. G. D. Miles, Wilkesbarre, Pa.	10 00
Rev. D. D. Smith	50 00
Member of Trinity Church, Columbus, Ohio, for library use	30 00
" " " " "	10 00
Rev. J. Ufford, Delaware, Ohio	5 00
Harcourt Parish, Gambier, Ohio	229 48
St. John's Church, Cleveland, Ohio	27 90
St. Paul's German Ch., "	7 72
St. Timothy's Church, Massillon, Ohio	27 00
Hon. G. Volney Dorsey, Columbus, "	50 00
Mrs. G. T. Bedell, Gambier, "	45 00
Mr. Turner, Mt. Vernon, "	5 00
Mrs. E. Cook, Sandusky, "	10 00
Rev. A M. Morrison, Gambier, " Cabinet Organ	300 00
Mrs. M. C. Kendal, Grand Rapids, Mich.	50 00
Chas. Alley, Co. C., Iowa	2 50
Rev. Mr. Wright, Boston, Mass.	10 00
Dr. D. Jayne, Philadelphia, Pa. Box of Medicine.	
Rev. Dr. Morse, Steubenville, Ohio. 170 books, for library.	
Rev. L. W. Bancroft, Gambier, " 18 " "	

1865.

Rt. Rev. Wm. B. Stevens, Philadelphia, Pa.	$ 50 00
Mrs. M. H. Brunot, Pittsburgh, Pa.	100 00

St. Andrew's Church, Philadelphia, Pa.	$250 00
St. Paul's " Chestnut Hill, Philadelphia, Pa.	98 00
Christ " Germantown, " "	12 00
Church of the Nativity, Philadelphia, Pa., S. S	25 00
Emmanuel Church, " "	23 50
Church of the Mediator, " "	50 00
Mrs. G., Greene Co., Pa.	2 50
Wm. Ball, Jr., Philadelphia, Pa.	20 00
Miss M. K. A. Stone, Philadelphia, Pa.	30 00
Two Ladies, " "	10 00
E. L. Bowman, " "	25 00
Christ Church, Brownsville, Pa., S. S.	10 00
St. Andrew's Church, Wilmington, Del.	40 00
Christ Church, Christiana, Del.	150 53
Emmanuel Church, Baltimore, Md.	100 00
St. Peter's " " " by a member	100 00
" " " "	34 40
Carrie S. Hill, " "	10 00
St. James' Church, New London, Conn.	60 00
St. John's " Hartford, "	80 00
" " " " by a lady	5 00
Christ " " "	53 00
Grace " Manchester, "	20 00
Two persons, Middletown, "	2 50
Church of the Redeemer, Providence, R.I.	50 45
St. Mark's Church, Warren, "	21 00
Rev. Dr. Packard, Lawrence, Mass.	30 00
St. John's Church, Jamaica Plains, Mass.	50 00
Miss Stocker, Boston, "	5 00
Mrs. Rand, " "	20 00
E. S. Rand, Emmanuel Church, Boston, Mass.	60 00
Rev. G. L. Locke, Boston, Mass.	5 00
Missionary Society, Mass.	50 00
Trinity Church, Boston, Mass., a member	5 00
" " "	32 50
St. John's Church, Portsmouth, N. H	37 00
St. Paul's " Concord, "	51 73
Mrs. Eames, " "	5 00
St. John's Church, Newtown, L. I	86 00
Christ " Gardiner, Me.	54 57
Gift of a departed Christian, Gardiner, Me.	50 00
L. L. Pitkin, Rochester, N. Y	25 00
John H. Swift, New York, "	25 00
Christ Church, Sodus Ridge, N. Y	1 00

W. B. Jackson, Utica, New York	$ 25 00
Church of the Evangelists, Oswego, N. Y.	25 00
Christ Church, Brooklyn, N. Y.	300 00
St. Ann's Church, Brooklyn, N. Y.	10 00
C. G. A. Johnson, Grandville, Ohio	50 00
Rev. J. G. Auer, Gambier, "	50 00
Grace Church, Sandusky, " by a lady	30 00
St. Peter's Church, Delaware, "	5 00
" " " " a member	10 00
All Saints' Church, Portsmouth "	62 50
Rev. H. Tullidge, Norwalk, "	5 00
St. John's Church, Cincinnati, "	75 00
Rev. John Boyd, Marietta, "	10 00
Rev. W. Bower, Newark, "	3 00
A German friend, Cleveland. "	1 00
J. B. Johnson, Grandville, "	10 00
Rev. Dr. Anderson, Columbus. " Trinity Church	20 00
G. T. Odiorne, Cincinnati, "	25 00
Grace Church, Sandusky, "	20 00
St. Paul's Church, Mt. Vernon, " S. S.	26 78
" " Norwalk, "	20 00
Trinity " Columbus, " a member	20 00
All Saints' " Portsmouth, " S. S.	125 00
Church of the Epiphany, Urbana	11 00
St. Peter's Church, Gallipolis, Ohio	21 00
Lady, in Worthington, "	25 00
Bexley Hall Missionary Society, Gambier, Ohio	15 54
M——, Delaware, Ohio	3 50
Christ Church, Dayton, Ohio	25 00
Mrs. E. S. Haynes, Cincinnati, Ohio	100 00
Bishop Bedell and Sister, Gambier, Ohio	100 00
Bishop Bedell and Mrs. Julia Bedell, Gambier, Ohio	500 00
Rev. R. L. Chittenden, 42d Reg. O. V. I.	15 00
Rev. H. L. Clarkson, Chicago, Ill., St. James' Church	5 00
Thomas Bidwell, Wentwell, "	30 00
J. M. L., Co. I., 77th Ill. Vols., New Orleans	5 00
St. John's Church, Chicago, Ill., 2 members.	5 00
Church of the Advent, San Francisco, Cal.	200 00
Gentleman and his wife	50 00
Ascension Church, Frankfort, Ky.	28 00
A	10 00
From a house mother	2 00
Bishop Whipple	10 00
M	5 00

Students...	$ 1 25
C. F...	20 00
Trinity Church, Washington, D. C., S. S.................	75 00
Rev. J. Roch, Valparaiso, Ind...........................	5 00
Rev. J. Coch, St. Joseph's, Mo..........................	5 00
Rev. S. D. Hinman, Dacotah Indian Mission...............	9 00
Moccasins, from Dacotah Indian Congregation.	
Anonymous...	50 00
Society for Increase of Ministry........................	200 00
A friend of solid foundations...........................	500 00
Female Prayer Book Society, Phila., Pa....24 Prayer Books.	

RECEIPTS OF THE MISSION HOUSE, PHILADELPHIA, PA.,

FROM JUNE 1, 1866.

P. Neff, Esq., Treasurer of the Gambier M. H., Ohio......	$ 2,476 98
Jay Cooke, Esq., Philadelphia, Pa........................	10,000 00
St. Stephen's Church, Harrisburg, Pa., Bible Class.......	12 00
Church of the Mediator, Philadelphia, Pa., S. S..........	72 04
" " " " "	150 00
Miss E. N. Biddle, " "	57 00
Church of the Nativity, " "	251 00
" " Covenant, " "	150 00
" " Advent, " " S. S..........	200 00
" " " " " Miss Baker,	
Scholarship..	300 00
Christ Church, Germantown, Philadelphia, Pa.............	178 13
Church of the Epiphany, " "	227 00
" " " " " Mission S. S.	55 00
" The Saviour, West " "	320 20
St. Andrew's Church, " "	200 00
Church of the Holy Trinity, West Chester, "	25 00
St. Luke's Church, Philadelphia, Pa......................	200 00
St. Philip's " " " a member...........	20 00
Grace " Great Bend, "	7 08
St. Peter's " Phœnixville, "	21 63
" " " " S. S................	17 28
B. G. Godfrey, Philadelphia. "	100 00
Rev. Jas. Saul, " "	25 00

St. Clement's Ch., Philadelphia, Pa.	$ 16 35
St. Mark's " " "	115 00
Holy Trinity " " " a member	20 00
Mary K. A. Stone, " "	100 00
Mrs. C. A. Ivens, " "	5 00
Julia A. Wiltberger, " "	5 00
Thomas T. Lee, " "	5 00
Miss Ella Bowman, Lancaster, "	100 00
Rev. L. C. Newman, Philadelphia, Pa.	17 00
W. Ball (in goods)	5 75
St. Paul's Church, Cheltenham, Pa., furniture	450 00
Rev. Mr. Kellogg, (a lady), "	2 00
Miss M. Bowman, "	200 00
Jas. T. Allen, "	20 00
Edwin Manly	10 00
Trinity Church, Bergen Pt., N. J., S. S.	20 00
St. Matthew's Church, Jersey City, N. J., Miss'y articles	40 00
Trinity Church, Columbus, Ohio	25 00
Mrs. J. E. Bates, " "	10 00
St. Paul's Church, Norwalk, Ohio	15 00
All Saints' Church, Portsmouth, Ohio, S. S.	187 50
Christ Church, Springfield, " "	36 28
Grace Church, Sandusky, "	44 06
Rev. J. G. Auer, "	15 00
Harcourt Parish, Gambier, "	202 00
George Bower, Newark, Ohio	5 00
Mrs. J. B. Smith, Gambier, "	24 50
" " " " Ladies of Gambier	3 00
St. Paul's Church, Akron, Ohio, Thanksgiving offering of members	35 00
Calvary Church, Clifton, Ohio	50 00
St. Paul's " Newburyport, Mass.	20 00
Missionary Society "	200 00
Christ Church, Christiana, Del.	74 26
" " " a member	100 00
Rob't H. Ives, Providence, R. I.	500 00
St. Luke's Church, Rochester, N. Y. (a little girl)	4 50
Miss J. K. Bloomfield, Oswego, "	2 00
St. Ann's Church, Brooklyn, "	75 00
S. B. Caldwell, New York, "	100 00
G. L. Rose, Geneva, "	10 00
A Friend	8 00
Society for Increase of Ministry	150 00
St. Paul's Church, Virgenus, Vt., S. S.	5 00
Secretary Board Missions, New York	592 55

Miss Ellen Watkinson	$50 00
J. P. M.	25 00
Michigan	8 00
J. W. B., from the Episcopalian	20 00
Bishop Payne, Africa	52 00
Mrs. Dr. Vaughan, Philadelphia	Box of books.
Miss Foley	Box of books.
Mrs. J. L. Curtis	6 pieces of clothing.
Per Rev. Mr. Childs	5 tons of coal.

1867.

St. Luke's Church, Philadelphia, Pa., Coll.	$ 32 72
" " " from C. Wheeler	100 00
Church of the Saviour, West Philadelphia, Pa.	75 00
Rev. W. H. Hare, "	10 00
Church of the Crucifixion, "	9 30
Grace Church, "	30 00
St. Luke's Church, Philad'a, Pa.	150 00
" " " Per Rev. R. J. Parvin	70 00
St. Paul's Church, Cheltenham, Pa.	600 00
Church of the Mediator, Philadelphia, Pa.	300 00
N. P. S.	500 00
St. Paul's Church, Philadelphia, Pa.	325 00
St. Andrew's Church "	300 00
Church of the Epiphany, " Mission S. S.	50 00
" " " Coll.	65 40
" " "	545 00
St. Jude's Church, " S. S.	10 00
St. Stephen's Church, Harrisburg, Pa., Per A. C. M. S.	69 19
Church of the Holy Trinity, Philadelphia, Pa.	315 00
St. Matthew's Church, " Infant S. S.	13 59
Trinity Chapel, "	51 16
Church of Our Saviour, West "	168 56
St. Luke's Chapel, "	5 00
Church of the Nativity, "	125 00
C. P. B. Jeffries, "	100 00
Emmanuel Church, Philadelphia, Pa.	50 00
W. H. H. Roberts, "	10 00
Gloria Dei Church, "	300 00
Ascension Church, "	12 65
Calvary Church, Germantown, "	5 00
Grace Church, Mount Airy, "	25 00
St. Andrew's Church, West "	21 00
St. Mark's Church, Frankford "	301 19

Christ Church, Germantown, Philadelphia, Pa.	$100 00
A Friend in Germantown, Philadelphia, Pa.	100 00
Church of the Evangelists, Philadelphia, Pa.	37 67
Church of the Covenant, "	151 40
Ch. of the Advent, Philad'a, Pa., Miss Baker...Scholarship.	200 00
Grace Church, Great Bend, Pa.	2 50
Rev. Mr. Jerome, New Milford, Pa.	5 00
St. Mark's Church, New Milford, Pa.	2 00
Rev. D. D. Smith, Philadelphia, Pa.	50 00
Wm. Welsh, "	500 00
John Bohlen, "	100 00
Rev. A. M. Morrison, "	500 00
Rev. A. M. Morrison, "	600 00
Rev. B. B. Laycock, " for S. S.	47 00
Rev. Dr. Kellogg, " cash	7 00
Grace Church, " F. Miss. Society	50 00
M. K. A. S., "	20 00
Mrs. E. Ball, "	6 00
Lydia, "	2 00
Harriet Montgomery, "	3 00
Ch. of the Intercessor, "	12 42
Rev. Sam'l Hazlehurst, " Gift of a dying child	35 00
W. G. Morehead, "	300 00
Jay Cooke, "	300 00
Church of the Saviour, Philadelphia, Pa.	22 00
St. John's Church, York, Pa.	38 50
St. Andrew's Church, Wilmington, Del.	300 00
Christ Church, Christiana, Del.	70 00
Rev. G. Z. Gray, Bergen Pt., N. J.	20 00
St. Matthew's S. S., Bloomington, Ill.	70 00
A Friend, Boston, Mass.	10 00
Foreign Committee, New York	346 38
——— ———, Bridgeport, Conn.	20 00
Christ Church, " "	52 00
F. E. Richmond, Providence, R. I.	50 00
Mass. Miss. Society	50 00
St. Ann's Church, Brooklyn, N. Y.	225 00
Pitt Cooke, New York	50 00
Miss J. K. Bloomfield, Oswego, N. Y.	1 00
E. W. Dunham, New York	100 00
Church of the Mediator, New York	49 50
Stewart Brown, New York	300 00
Rev. W. L. Postlethwaite, Brooklyn, New York	100 00
J. B. Sheafe, New York	1000 00

Rev. L. H. Sherwood, Lyons, New York	$32 00
W. B. Jackson, Utica, New York	20 00
St. Peter's Church, Smyrna, Del	20 38
Rev. S. D. Hinman, Nebraska, Miss'y	25 00
A. M. Treadwell, Madison, Morris Co., N. J	25 00
———, Newark, N. J	10 00
St. Paul's Church, Norwalk, Ohio	14 50
All Saints' Church, Portsmouth, Ohio	187 50
Grace Church, Sandusky, Ohio	130 00
Grace Church, Sandusky, Ohio, Per A. M. C. M. S.	60 00
Trinity Church, Columbus, Ohio, S. S.	25 00
St. John's Church, Cincinnati, Ohio	50 00
Rosse Chapel, Gambier, Ohio	36 01
St. Paul's Church, Mt. Vernon, Ohio	38 17
German S. S., Nashotah	1 36
St. Peter's Church, Baltimore, Md	125 50
Emmanuel Church, Baltimore, Md., Per A. C. M. S.	25 00
Ev. Ed. Society, Philadelphia, Pa	150 00
Mrs. W. J. Rees, Lancaster, Ohio	Box of clothing.
St. Paul's Church, Miss. Soc., Boston, Mass.	" "
H. L. Rehn, Philadelphia, Pa	Books for Library.

1868.

Christ Church, Germantown, Philadelphia, Pa., per Board Missions	$200 25
Christ Church, Germantown, Philadelphia, Pa	50 00
St. Paul's Church, " S. S.	210 73
Church of the Mediator, "	150 00
Church of the Nativity, "	100 00
Church of the Epiphany, "	550 00
J. S. Whitney, "	20 00
Grace Church, Philadelphia, Pa., F. Miss. Soc	50 00
Grace Church, " Male Bible Class	20 00
Church of the Covenant, Philadelphia, Pa., per S. S.	300 00
All Saints' Church, "	37 80
Church of the Crucifixion, Philadelphia, Pa	13 75
Miss E. Clement, Germantown, "	25 00
St. Stephen's Church, Wilkesbarre, Pa	78 46
Church of the Holy Trinity, Philadelphia, Pa	300 00
Wm. Welsh, Philadelphia, Pa	20 00
Mrs. S. Simes, "	5 00
A. Wheeler, "	25 00
Two Friends, "	110 00
Jay Cooke, "	334 00

Widow of a Clergyman, Philadelphia, Pa................. $	25 00
C. B. Durborow, "	100 00
Wm. G. Morehead, "	300 00
Miss Mary Bowman, "	100 00
Samuel G. DeCourcy, "	100 00
E. J. A., "	10 00
Church of the Advent, " Miss Baker, Scholarship.	100 00
St. Paul's Church, Cheltenham, Philadelphia, Pa.........	14 60
Grace Church, Mt. Airy, Pa., Lenten offering............	54 95
" Honesdale, Pa.....................	25 00
Church of the Saviour, West Philadelphia, Pa............	258 60
St. John's Church, York, Pa.............................	78 00
St. Philip's " Summit Hill, Carbon Co., Pa., S. S....	43 54
Evangelical Ed. Soc., Philadelphia, Pa...................	675 00
Christ Church, Christiana, per Board of Missions.........	37 43
" " by a member..................	106 00
Christ Church, Troy, N. Y...............................	40 00
St. John's Church, Georgetown, D. C.....................	36 00
Christ Church, per A. C. M. S., Bay Ridge, L. I., S. S.....	117 44
Grace " " Sandusky, Ohio, "	60 00
St. James' Church, Worcester, Ohio, S. S.................	5 51
Rev. L. L. Holden, " " "	4 49
St. Andrew's Church, Wilmington, Del....................	185 48
" " " " S. S...............	55 00
" " " " Calvary Chapel.....	59 52
Grace Church, Georgetown, D. C........................	10 00
All Saints' Church, Portsmouth, Ohio....................	102 50
St. Peter's " Baltimore, Md......................	111 00
Christ Church, Brooklyn, N. Y., S. S.....................	50 00
St. Ann's " " "	5 00
" " " " per A. C. M. S..........	300 00
" " " " coll....................	5 00
St. John's " Somerville, New Jersey..................	23 00
Trinity " Mt. Holly, "	33 00
" " " " S. S...............	22 43
St. Paul's Church, Boston, Mass.........................	100 00
Trinity Chapel, Newark, New Jersey.....................	14 57
" " " S. S...................	10 68
St. John's Church, L. I., S. S...................	35 23
St. Peter's " Smyrna, Del. S. S.....	50 00
Church of Our Saviour, Brooklyn, N. Y., S. S............	161 19
Rev. L. H. Sherwood, Lyons, N. Y......................	25 00
St. Peter's Church, Baltimore, Md., S. S..................	150 00
Grace Church, Providence, R. I.........................	162 42
Stewart Brown, New York, per A. C. M. Soc.............	300 00

Philadelphia Bible Society................One Large Bible.
Advancement Society...............Large Prayer Book.
St. Stephen's Church, Wilkesbarre. Four Boxes Provisions.
Grace Church, Mt. Airy.............One Box Provisions.
A Friend.......................Books for the Library.

June 21, Evangelical Educational Society.................	$200 00
July 7, Men's Missionary Society Church of the Mediator.	37 50
" 7, Women's " " " "	37 50
" 14, A. K. A. Stone, Cambridge, Mass................	25 00
" 16, Members of the Church of the Atonement, N. Y...	100 00
" 24, Ladies' Benevolent Society, St. Michael's, Bristol..	35 58
Aug. 1, St. Michael's, Trenton......................	68 58
" 13, Mrs. Rebecca Gumbes, Philadelphia..............	100 00
" 25, Collection by F. B. Whitney....................	100 00
" 31, Christ Church, Lonsdale, Rhode Island...........	59 85
Sep. 19, A. M. Tredwell, New York......................	25 00
" 21, Miss E. Clement, Germantown, (special)..........	100 00
" 24, Jay Cooke......................................	500 00
" 28, St. Mark's, New Milford, Pa.....................	7 50
" 28, George Boyd, Philadelphia......................	25 00
" 30, Miss Mary Bowman, (special)....................	150 00
Oct. 1, John Bohlen, (special).........................	100 00
" 1, Collection by Mr. Whitney.....................	26 00
" 1, S. S. All Saints', Portsmouth....................	40 00
" 2, William Welsh, (special).......................	100 00
" 3, A. Whitney & Sons, (special)...................	100 00
" 7, C. P. B. Jefferies, (special)....................	100 00
" 7, Christ Church, Towanda, Pa.....................	22 48
" 7, Holy Trinity, West Chester.....................	54 53
" 7, N. Parker Shortridge, Philadelphia, (special)......	100 00
" 13, A. J. Drexel, (special)...........................	100 00
" 14, Christ Church, Westerly, Rhode Island...........	145 00
" 14, S. S. " " " "	30 00
" 16, Grace Church, Great Bend, Pa..................	3 00
" 29, Church of the Nativity, Philadelphia, (special).....	100 00
" 29, Grace Church, Sandusky, Ohio..................	50 00
" 29, Anonymous, per C. E. Lex......................	5 00
" 29, St. Peter's Phœnixville.........................	27 12
Nov. 3, W. J. Vaux...................................	50 00
" 3, C. B. Durborow, (special).......................	100 00
" 3, St. Peter's, Smyrna, Del........................	6 23
" 5, F. R. Brunot, Pittsburg, (special)...............	100 00
" 5, S. S. Grace Church, Sandusky, Ohio............	50 00
" 6, Church Advent, Philadelphia, Baker scholarship...	144 45
" 10, Men's Miss. So. Ch. Mediator, Philadelphia.......	37 50